Implementing
POSITIVE BEHAVIOR SUPPORT SYSTEMS
in Early Childhood and Elementary Settings

KANSAS TECHNICAL ASSISTANCE SYSTEM NETWORK
www.ksdetasn.org

Compliments of TASN

To all the administrators, staff, and students of the schools and programs who have allowed us to learn from them in their efforts to support all children. In particular, we thank the Special School District of St. Louis County, Columbia Public Schools, Central Missouri Head Start, Rockwood Public Schools Early Childhood Program, and our "research" schools: Parkade, Benton, Paxton-Keeley, Rock Bridge, Halls Ferry, Wedgewood Elementary Schools, Gentry Middle School, and Neuwoehner School.

Lists of Tables and Figures

Contents

For information:

Corwin Press
A SAGE Company
2455 Teller Road
Thousand Oaks, California 91320
www.corwinpress.com

SAGE India Pvt. Ltd.
B 1/I 1 Mohan Cooperative
    Industrial Area
Mathura Road, New Delhi 110 044
India

SAGE Ltd.
1 Oliver's Yard
55 City Road
London EC1Y 1SP
United Kingdom

SAGE Asia-Pacific Pte. Ltd.
33 Pekin Street #02–01
Far East Square
Singapore 048763

Printed in the United States of America

Library of Congress Cataloging-in-Publication Data

Implementing positive behavior support systems in early childhood and elementary settings/by Melissa Stormont . . . [et al.].
        p. cm.
Includes bibliographical references and index.
ISBN 978-1-4129-4055-9 (cloth)
ISBN 978-1-4129-4056-6 (pbk.)
    1. Behavior modification. 2. Problem children—Education (Early childhood)
3. Problem children—Education (Elementary) 4. Socialization. I. Stormont, Melissa.
II. Title.

LB1060.2.I47 2008
370.15'28—dc22   2007020452

This book is printed on acid-free paper.

        13   10   9   8   7   6   5   4

Acquisitions Editor:	Allyson P. Sharp
Editorial Assistant:	Mary Dang
Production Editor:	Cassandra Margaret Seibel
Copy Editor:	Marzie McCoy
Typesetter:	C&M Digitals (P) Ltd.
Proofreader:	Kristin Bergstad
Indexer:	Terri Corry
Cover Designer:	Scott Van Atta

Implementing
POSITIVE BEHAVIOR SUPPORT SYSTEMS
in Early Childhood and Elementary Settings

Melissa Stormont • Timothy J. Lewis
Rebecca Beckner • Nanci W. Johnson

CORWIN PRESS
A SAGE Company
Thousand Oaks, CA 91320

educators, school psychologists, counselors, behavioral consultants, para-professionals, and instructional aides. Unique features of this text include

- A research foundation to support PW/SW-PBS features.
- A presentation of systems structures that have to be in place to help support implementation.
- Professional development needs and processes.
- A focus on teams and unique school cultures to guide implementation of key features.
- A clear step-by-step description of how to implement key features.
- Case examples.
- A data-based problem-solving process.
- Implementation exemplars from preschool programs and elementary schools.
- A theme of teaching and using social errors to inform instruction.

Preface

This book provides teaching professionals with a positive and preventive approach for working with challenging behavior in young children. The importance of this text is clear as the number of children with behavior problems in schools is increasing and teachers do not feel prepared to work with challenging behavior in the classroom. The typical school response to problem behavior has been reactionary and punishment oriented. It is clear from the research that this approach does not work for children with behavior problems and, in fact, makes their behavior worse. The content of this book reflects a different means for working with problem behavior, which includes using a proactive, teaching-oriented approach. Children learn social behavior the same way they learn academic skills, and, accordingly, they need teachers to teach specific behavioral expectations.

The primary purpose of this book is to serve as a resource for professionals interested in or currently involved in establishing systems of programwide/schoolwide positive behavioral support (PW/SW-PBS). We are aware of no other book of this kind that will support programs and schools currently implementing systems of PW/SW-PBS with young children. This book includes the research foundation for PW/SW-PBS, the system pieces that have to be in place to support successful implementation, and a thorough description of each of the key features. The focus of this book is on establishing universal supports for all students on which more intense and individualized supports can be built for children with additional support needs.

This book can be a useful resource for any professional involved in supporting PW/SW-PBS, including administrators, general educators, special

Acknowledgments

The University of Missouri Center for School-wide Positive Behavior Support, supported in part by the Office of Special Education Programs, U.S. Department of Education (Grants H324T000021 and H326S030002).

The OSEP Center on Positive Behavioral Interventions and Supports (Grant H324X010015).

Corwin Press would also like to thank the following reviewers:

Polly White
Assistant Principal/Assistant Special Services Supervisor
Aumsville Elementary School
Aumsville, OR

Connie E. Radunzel
NBCT, Special Education
Lake Hills Elementary
Bellevue, WA

Mark Alter, PhD
Professor of Educational Psychology
New York University
New York, NY

Julia DeGarmo
Special Needs Preschool Teacher
Columbus Public Schools
Blacklick, OH

having their actions monitored on a regular basis, having regular opportunities for academic and social success, and having access to meaningful feedback that guides their behavior (Sugai & Lewis, 1996).

Unfortunately, not all children and youth have access to appropriate models, regular monitoring, regular academic and social success, and meaningful feedback. Instead, at-risk children's appropriate social experiences are best characterized as infrequent, haphazard, and trial-and-error learning experiences. In fact, children and youth who are at risk for developing or who already display antisocial behavior are an ever-increasing concern in American schools and communities. Teachers report that as many as one in five students displays acting-out, disruptive behaviors to the point at which intervention is necessary (Myers & Holland, 2000). A similar pattern is reported in early childhood settings. For example, young children who are at risk and educated in Head Start programs are reported to be significantly more physically aggressive than similar-age peers (Kupersmidt, Bryant, & Willoughby, 2000). Head Start teachers report that up to 40% of their students exhibit one or more problem behaviors on a daily basis (Willoughby, Kupersmidt, & Bryant, 2001). Further contributing to their risk, children with behavior problems also have deficits in appropriate social skills. Teachers agree that social skills such as self-management, basic problem solving, and getting along with others are necessary prerequisites for success in school (Stormont, Beckner, Mitchell, & Richter, 2005). However, many teachers also indicate that more and more children are not coming to school with the necessary skills for success (Odom, McConnell, & McEvoy, 1992; Stormont, 2007).

It is clear that educators struggle when trying to manage children's problem behavior in the classroom and when attempting to address missing social skills. Most feel unprepared to address children's social needs. The importance and urgency to develop appropriate patterns of social behavior among young children simply cannot be emphasized enough, and educators need to have both an understanding of this urgency and the tools for responding. It is clear that there is a link between relatively minor, nonviolent behaviors often seen in young children, such as disrespect and noncompliance, and later more serious patterns of problem behavior, including violent and aggressive acts (Heaviside, Rowand, Williams, & Farris, 1998; Tobin & Sugai, 1999; Tobin, Sugai, & Colvin, 1996). Unfortunately, educators continue to rely on traditional discipline tactics that focus on punishing problem behavior. However, research indicates that not only are traditional punishment-based discipline practices ineffective among high-risk students, but they actually increase, not decrease, rates of problem behavior (Mayer, 1995, 2001). In addition to the overreliance on punishment to respond to problem

1

A Proactive Approach to Behavior Management

C onsider the following: "If antisocial behavior is not changed by the end of Grade 3, it should be treated as a chronic condition much like diabetes. That is, it cannot be cured but can be managed with the appropriate supports and continuing intervention" (Walker, Colvin, & Ramsey, 1995, p. 6). As the statement indicates, families, schools, and community agencies have a window of opportunity in which to make a significant impact on children's social behavior. However, the statement does not suggest that beyond Grade 3 educators give up on children with challenging behavior; rather, a parallel to diabetes is especially relevant. People with diabetes can lead normal, healthy lives provided they monitor and adjust their blood sugar, monitor their diet, and exercise. If they fail to do any of the three, they face more serious health complications and perhaps even death. If schools are to effectively prevent chronic challenging behavior and support those students who do not receive early intensive and comprehensive interventions, they must monitor the students' "diet and blood sugar" and provide the "exercise" to maintain mental health and prevent more serious challenges.

Fortunately, most children and youth adjust reasonably well to challenges. These children and youth acquire the necessary skills to function in our society through support from school, family, peer, and community experiences. Success is associated with having appropriate models available,

Rebecca Beckner is an early childhood behavior consultant with the public schools in Columbia, Missouri. She has been a family and individual counselor and has owned a child care center for 10 years, specializing in the care of children with behavioral concerns. Ms. Beckner currently participates in the evaluation of young children in the area of social-emotional-behavioral functioning and serves children with severe behavior problems and their families. She also facilitates several local programwide positive behavior support teams in the public schools, Head Start, and community day care facilities. Ms. Beckner has 20 years of experience consulting with teachers on behavior management and providing workshop and inservice training to teaching staff and parents on subjects such as positive behavior supports, social skills, strategies for supporting children with significant behavioral difficulties, resiliency, and communicating with parents. She is a certified trainer of programwide positive behavior support and has traveled throughout the country supporting teams as they implement the approach. Ms. Beckner is also working on her dissertation at the University of Missouri (special education, behavior disorders), which focuses on implementing the PBS approach to improve at-risk behavior of preschool children. Ms. Beckner is teaching courses on early childhood assessment and working with families.

Nanci W. Johnson is currently a positive behavior support facilitator for the Columbia, Missouri, Public Schools. She previously worked as part of the Missouri Positive Behavior Support Initiative, collaborating to develop state training materials, conducting school-based research, and providing consultation both in and out of the state. Dr. Johnson has taught parenting education, preschool, kindergarten, first-grade, as well as college-level course work. She has a special interest in systems-based school change, development of communities of practice to support effective instructional practices, and instructional leadership.

About the Authors

Melissa Stormont has been involved in special education and psychology for more than 15 years. She has worked to support children with behavioral problems as a teacher and behavioral consultant and through teaching teachers and conducting research in higher education. Currently, Dr. Stormont is an associate professor in special education at the University of Missouri. Dr. Stormont has published extensive research related to the educational and social needs of young children who are vulnerable for failure, including children with behavior problems, those with attention deficit hyperactivity disorder, and children who have limited resources as a result of poverty. Dr. Stormont's research has included a focus on family and school factors that contribute to risk and resiliency. She has published more than 30 articles and book chapters in these areas.

Timothy J. Lewis has been involved in special education for more than 20 years. He has taught students with emotional and behavioral disorders in high school, elementary school, and self-contained psychiatric settings. At present, Dr. Lewis is professor and associate dean for research, development, and graduate studies at the University of Missouri. Dr. Lewis has been involved with developing schoolwide systems of behavioral support for more than 15 years. He has worked directly with school teams around the world, has secured several federal grants to support his research and demonstration efforts, and is a frequent contributor to the professional literature examining various aspects of positive behavior support. His specialty areas include social skill instruction, functional assessment, and proactive schoolwide discipline systems.

behavior, teachers of young children also report that they feel unprepared to address problem behavior in more proactive ways (Stormont, Lewis, & Covington, 2005).

This combination of (a) increasing numbers of children starting school without critical socially acceptable skills needed for success, (b) the correlation between minor problem behavior in young children and later chronic severe patterns, and (c) the continued reliance on punishment to address problem behaviors has resulted in an increase in violent and aggressive acts among young adults to the point at which former Surgeon General C. Everett Koop declared it an epidemic (Koop & Lundberg, 1992). At issue is a disconnect between student learning history before entering school and during the early school years (i.e., their experiences and what they learned from them) and the assumptions educators make about that learning history. In essence, educational discipline strategies assume that all students have been taught appropriate social behavior and find that school reinforces such behavior. For example, the practice of in-school detention assumes that (a) students know what to do instead of the inappropriate behavior that landed them in detention and (b) students would rather be in the classroom (i.e., they find the classroom reinforcing) than in detention, thereby increasing the likelihood they monitor their behavior to avoid being removed in the future. For many of the students we work with, this is simply not the case. The remainder of this chapter provides a brief overview of the importance of factoring in learning history when developing comprehensive systems of behavior support. Based on students' learning history patterns that place them at risk, recommendations for addressing social problems in preschool and early elementary school are reviewed. Finally, an overview of schoolwide and programwide positive behavior support (PW/SW-PBS) is provided with supporting research to date.

THE IMPORTANCE OF UNDERSTANDING STUDENTS' PAST LEARNING EXPERIENCES

At the start of each school year, most teachers will assess prior student learning to match students to the curriculum. In some instances, the teacher must reteach prior concepts before starting the students within their grade-level curriculum. At other times, the teacher determines the students are farther along than expected and can skip beginning sections of the curriculum. In both cases, the teacher does not make assumptions about prior learning and relies on assessments as an integral part in matching instruction to students' current performance levels. In the former case, the teacher does not punish the students for not being at the expected level, even though he or she may be thinking "they should know this by now." In both cases, *the teacher teaches* to ensure that students have the needed skills. Again, the teacher teaches. It is essential to follow the same logic in designing social behavior curriculum, more commonly known as discipline or behavior management. Teachers should not make assumptions about what the children "should know by now"; rather, they should assess for prior knowledge and adjust curriculum and supports accordingly. In both the academic and the behavior cases, making assumptions about what students should know and implementing curriculum independent of student prior knowledge will result in academic and behavioral struggles. Continued academic and behavioral struggles across those critical early years of development often result in the development of lifelong learning and behavioral challenges.

Research conducted to understand the most extreme behavioral challenges, students who display antisocial behavior, provides a great example of the disconnect between a clearly learned pattern of social interaction that places children on a path toward a lifetime of antisocial behavior (e.g., school dropout, incarceration, violence, substance abuse) and assumptions about what students "should know by now" within schools (Patterson, 1982; Walker, Ramsey, & Gresham, 2004). Children are not born antisocial; they learn to become antisocial through social interactions with others. In essence, students at high risk for antisocial behavior learn to interact socially using what most would deem inappropriate behaviors through interactions with significant others in the home or community. Unfortunately, the inappropriate behaviors allow them to get their needs met and are often supported in the home, thereby maintaining the negative, or antisocial, behavior pattern over time. Basically, at-risk children's behavior is maintained and strengthened by the principles of negative reinforcement (Box 1.1). Overall, children who are at risk for antisocial behavior are typically motivated to avoid aversive outcomes as opposed to the typically developing child, who learns to develop patterns of behavior to receive positive reinforcement. Hence, when an educator threatens or implements the loss of recess or suspension (an aversive response for most children), not only will it not decrease problem behavior but it actually may make it worse because the educator is providing one more learning example of an adult attempting to control behavior through negative reinforcement. In other words, by failing to factor in the child's learning history to understand what governs his or her behavior and simply instituting what works for most kids, not only will we fail to alter the problem behavior but we will make it worse.

BOX 1.1
The Development of Antisocial Behavior

Most typically developing children learn through early interactions with caregivers to use socially appropriate skills to get their needs met. This pattern of interactions is governed by the principles of **positive reinforcement**. The principles of positive reinforcement indicate that when a behavior is contingently followed by an object or event individuals find reinforcing, they are more likely to continue to use that behavior in the future. For example, most children learn to ask politely for an item ("Please pass the juice") and reinforce those who comply ("Thanks!"). Through repeated experiences, children learn that by using certain skills (e.g., asking politely, saying thanks) they get their needs met (e.g., the cup of juice) in ways significant others find important (e.g., a parent praises the child for using good manners, another reinforcing event that ultimately becomes just as important as getting the basic need met). On the basis of these early learning experiences, most children find social praise given by adults, which is commonly found in school settings (e.g., smiles, verbal praise, or good marks), reinforcing and continue to use appropriate social behaviors.

Children who display antisocial behavior also learn to get their needs met; however, their behavior is typically governed by the principles of **negative reinforcement** (Patterson, 1982). Negative reinforcement also increases the likelihood of using specific future behaviors, but does so by the presentation of objects or events that individuals find aversive. If individuals comply with requests or social demands, the aversive is taken away. For example, when children ask parents for candy in the grocery store checkout line and parents say "No," children then begin to throw a tantrum, in other words an aversive. If parents comply (give the candy), children take away the aversive (the tantrum stops). In this case, the child has negatively reinforced the parent in that in the future when the child hears "No" and throws a tantrum, the parent is likely to comply with the initial request. Taking the example a step farther, we also know that children are likely to experience an aversive event once they have left the store, such as physical punishment or loss of privileges for throwing the tantrum. The result is a coercive cycle whereby children learn a set of social skills that involves presenting aversives to get their needs met and engaging in behaviors to avoid encountering aversives presented by others (vs. socially appropriate behavior to gain positive reinforcement from others; Patterson, 1982; Walker et al., 2004).

In addition to the environmental risk factors just mentioned (e.g., reinforcing inappropriate behavior), many children are vulnerable to social problems given their unique needs or disabilities (Stormont, 2007). For example, children with learning disabilities and attention deficit hyperactivity disorder also enter elementary settings without the same set of social skills as their same-age peers. In these cases, characteristics related to their disabilities and disorders have contributed to their social immaturity. Even though the foundations for their deficits are often not linked as tightly to their early learning experiences, their needs for social behavior supports are the same as those of children with early antisocial patterns.

RECOMMENDATIONS FROM THE FIELD

The need for effective strategies that simultaneously address current behavior problems and build a system of early intervention has been firmly established (Kamps, Kravits, Rauch, Kamps, & Chung, 2000; Kamps, Kravits, Stolze, & Swaggart, 1999). Fortunately, research has identified the necessary components of comprehensive systems that both prevent and address social behavior challenges (e.g., Peacock Hill Working Group, 1991; Walker et al., 1996; Webster-Stratton, 1997). Effective systems of behavioral support move beyond false assumptions of children's prior learning histories and include direct instruction, practice, and monitoring of social behavior. Research indicates that schools and communities can successfully reduce challenging behavior when a proactive prevention and early intervention program is implemented (e.g., Conduct Problems Prevention Research Group, 1992; Cotton, 1999; Elliot, 1994a, 1994b; Gresham, Sugai, & Horner, 2001; Sugai et al., 2000; Tolan & Guerra, 1994; Walker et al., 1996). Box 1.2 highlights research-based practices that have proven effective for reducing problem behavior while increasing appropriate behavior.

BOX 1.2
Research-Based Strategies to Prevent
and Address Problem Social Behavior

- Parent training to increase positive interactions, active supervision of children, and active participation in the child's education, thereby breaking the cycle of coercive interactions.
- Creating and adopting effective academic and preacademic curricula, particularly preliteracy and literacy skills, to ensure that children are successful learners, increase self-esteem, and reduce problem behavior.
- Direct and planned social skills instruction designed to teach specific social behavior that, when displayed by the student, results in positive judgments of social competence from peers and adults.
- Developing comprehensive schoolwide preventive behavior management strategies. Unfortunately, as indicated previously, schools and preschool programs do not routinely put effective proactive practices in place for many reasons. A promising solution for problem behavior is the systemic organization of these and other research-validated practices into systems referred to as *schoolwide positive behavior support* (SW-PBS).

PROGRAMWIDE/SCHOOLWIDE POSITIVE BEHAVIOR SUPPORT

SW-PBS is the implementation of behavioral support strategies, along a continuum of intensity, through a process that is focused on social behavior instruction, guided by data-based decision making, and consistently implemented across school environments (Sugai et al., 2000). The extension of SW-PBS to preschool settings has been referred to as programwide positive behavior support (PW-PBS). Preschool programs have been defined as early childhood programs that serve children ages three to five years (or kindergarten entry; Stormont, Lewis, & Beckner, 2005). Key features of PW-PBS are the same as those in SW-PBS, but implementers within preschool systems acknowledge that preschool classrooms in early childhood programs are often placed in several buildings or locations, and instructional and support strategies need to be adapted because of developmental considerations (Stormont, Lewis, & Beckner, 2005). SW-PBS or PW-PBS is not a packaged curriculum or "cookbook" approach to preventing problem behaviors; rather, it is a comprehensive *process* that uses multiple research-supported practices that are carefully matched to presenting problems. This process also places great emphasis on the necessary systems that must be in place to support sustained use.

CONTINUUM OF SUPPORTS AND KEY FEATURES

An important component of PW/SW-PBS is the adoption of a continuum of behavioral supports that acknowledges the simple fact that, like academic instruction, students will need differing levels of behavioral intervention and supports to be successful in school. Within the continuum are three levels of support. The first level focuses on primary prevention or **universal** behavioral and academic, or preacademic, supports. Here the focus is on prevention of problem behaviors, providing early intervention for those at risk and creating environments that will lead to improved small-group and individual intervention outcomes. Universal strategies lay the foundation and serve as the core focus of the PW/SW-PBS system. Key features of universal supports are

- Clear, positively stated schoolwide or programwide behavioral expectations that are generated and directly taught by the teaching staff.

- Consistent acknowledgment of student use and mastery of expectations.
- Application of an instructional focus in response to student problem behavior.
- Systematic use of consistent consequences for problem behavior.

Universal supports are further adapted to meet the unique needs of nonclassroom settings, such as playgrounds and cafeterias, and individual classrooms. Research has shown that approximately 80% to 85% of students will respond to proactive universal supports, display the desired appropriate behavior, and have few behavioral problems (Horner & Sugai, 2005; Lewis, Newcomer, Trussell, & Richter, 2006).

The second level of PW/SW-PBS focuses on the 10% to 15% of students who continue to display problem behaviors even with universal supports firmly in place (Sugai, Horner, Lewis, & Cheney, 2002). Through the use of data decision rules, students are identified early, before problem behaviors become intense and chronic, and receive secondary or **small-group/targeted** supports such as small-group social skill instruction, academic or preacademic supports, and self-management strategies (Hawken & Horner, 2003).

The final, tertiary level of support is **intensive or individualized**. Approximately 5% to 7% of students will require highly individualized behavior support programs based on a comprehensive behavioral assessment (Lewis, Sugai, & Colvin, 1998). These students typically display serious and chronic behavioral challenges, at times necessitating the inclusion of special education, mental health, or family services. Figure 1.1 provides a graphic representation of the PW/SW-PBS continuum along with expected percentages of students commonly found at each level within a typical elementary school (Horner & Sugai, 2005).

Most schools and programs can identify a similar range of supports currently in place. That is, most students respond to the general discipline approach of the school (universal), some receive small-group supports delivered perhaps by the counselor or other specialists, and a few receive individualized supports through services such as special education. The difference within PW/SW-PBS schools is that, across all three levels of the continuum, every level of support is grounded within the framework of the universal system. Within most schools, although there may be several levels of behavioral support in place, teachers and other adults are hard-pressed to identify those students who receive additional supports; the objectives of the specialized service, activities, or focus within the specialized support; and their role in promoting maintenance and generalization. By building a connected continuum, *everyone* in the school or program is aware of how each level of support is connected to the universal system.

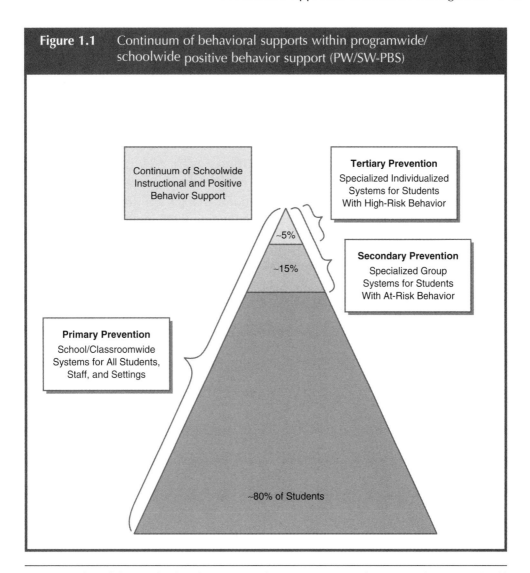

Figure 1.1 Continuum of behavioral supports within programwide/ schoolwide positive behavior support (PW/SW-PBS)

Continuum of Schoolwide Instructional and Positive Behavior Support

Tertiary Prevention
Specialized Individualized Systems for Students With High-Risk Behavior

~5%

~15%

Secondary Prevention
Specialized Group Systems for Students With At-Risk Behavior

Primary Prevention
School/Classroomwide Systems for All Students, Staff, and Settings

~80% of Students

SOURCE Adapted from *School-Wide Positive Behavior Support: Implementers' Blueprint and Self-Assessment,* by OSEP Center on Positive Behavioral Interventions and Supports, 2004, Eugene, OR: Author.

In other words, every small-group and individual intervention uses the universal set of behavioral expectations to increase the likelihood of maintenance and generalization and to provide repeated opportunities for student practice and adult acknowledgment.

To implement a functioning continuum of behavioral supports, there are three interconnected essential features of PW/SW-PBS: (a) use of empirically validated practices to support students, (b) adoption of specific behavioral supports based on data, and (c) development of systemic supports for the adults within the environment to ensure correct and sustained implementation (Lewis & Sugai, 1999; see Figure 1.2). The systematic support needs are driven by teams that include representatives of the school or program who drive and monitor system implementation and determine needs for support. Teams monitor the use of research-based practices and drive the data collection process. The type of data needed is determined by the team; data are used to make decisions regarding progress and needs for support. Box 1.3 provides a typical example of how the PW/SW-PBS process plays out during a team meeting. Each of these three features works simultaneously to characterize the true essence of PW/SW-PBS.

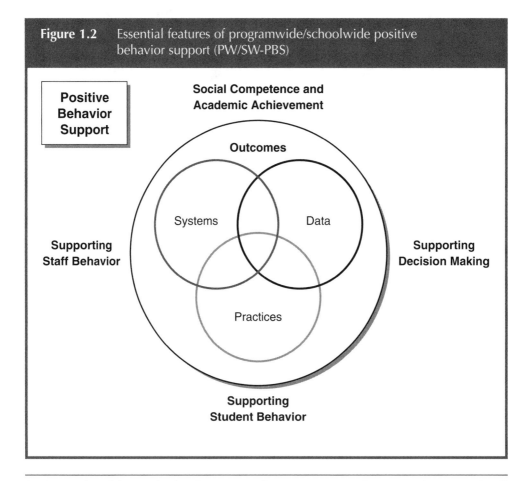

Figure 1.2 Essential features of programwide/schoolwide positive behavior support (PW/SW-PBS)

Positive Behavior Support

Social Competence and Academic Achievement

Outcomes

Systems

Data

Practices

Supporting Staff Behavior

Supporting Decision Making

Supporting Student Behavior

SOURCE Adapted from *School-Wide Positive Behavior Support: Implementers' Blueprint and Self-Assessment,* by OSEP Center on Positive Behavioral Interventions and Supports, 2004, Eugene, OR: Author.

BOX 1.3
SW-PBS Example of Using Data to Identify Needed Practices and Supports

During a recent SW-PBS meeting at an elementary school, the team noticed an increase in behavioral problems right after the lunch recess. Being good problem solvers, they immediately started proposing possible interventions such as reteaching playground expectations or increasing supervision, which are both research-based practices to address playground behavior. However, on further examination of the data, the team discovered that students weren't displaying problems on the playground; rather, they were displaying problem behaviors within specialist classrooms (e.g., art, music, physical education), which occurred right after lunch recess. The team then proposed, and implemented, an intervention that consisted of the classroom teachers escorting their classes to the specialist, taking five to ten minutes at the start of the class to review the behavioral expectations alongside the specialist, and then leaving. Behavioral infractions fell to near-zero levels the remainder of the school year during this critical transition period. The team followed the essential steps of (a) using data to identify where, when, and what the problem of concern was; (b) implementing a proven practice (reteach and review expectations) based on the identification of the specific problem revealed through data analysis; and (c) providing systemic support to their colleagues, in this case the specialist teachers, by agreeing to give up some of their planning time to implement the proposed intervention.

In summary, the key features of PW/SW-PBS include (a) the formation of a school or program team, (b) the creation of a continuum of supports, (c) the implementation of key features to support children's use of appropriate behavior across all school settings, (c) consistent implementation by all adults within the school or program, and (d) the use of data to inform every part of the process. We discuss these and other features in depth throughout the text.

SUPPORT FOR PROGRAMWIDE AND SCHOOLWIDE POSITIVE BEHAVIOR SUPPORT

Research to date has demonstrated that, when schoolwide universal systems of support are in place, schools report a reduction of up to 60% in behavioral infractions (Horner & Sugai, 2005) and improved levels of social behavior for both typically developing and at-risk students (Safran & Oswald, 2003). For example, within one school year, Taylor-Greene et al. (1997) reported a 42% reduction in office discipline referrals in a middle school and maintenance of the overall reduction in subsequent school years (Taylor-Greene & Kartub, 2000). This maintenance effect (i.e., the 2000 data represented a completely new group of students) is a critical finding of this research because it highlights the importance of building systems of support that continually teach and practice school expectations. Nakasato (2000) also reported significant decreases across six elementary schools following the implementation of SW-PBS. Scott (2001) extended the support for SW-PBS by showing reductions in both minor behavioral infractions and more severe infractions that resulted in a 65% reduction of out-of-school suspensions.

Extending universal supports to nonclassroom settings, Lewis et al. (1998) demonstrated that, through the combination of social skill instruction on how behavioral expectations apply to specific settings and an increase in proactive supervision, an elementary school was able to reduce problem behaviors in the cafeteria, in hallways, and on the playground. A follow-up study further demonstrated that, through the same combination of instruction and supervision, another elementary school was able to significantly reduce problems during three separate recess periods (Lewis, Colvin, & Sugai, 2000). Other research has also demonstrated that the application of universal SW-PBS can reduce problem behaviors in nonclassroom settings, including hallways, buses, and playgrounds (Colvin, Sugai, Good, & Lee, 1997; Kartub, Taylor-Greene, March, & Horner, 2000; Lewis, Powers, Kelk, & Newcomer, 2002; Putnam, Handler, Ramirez-Platt, & Luiselli, 2003; Todd, Haugen, Anderson, & Spriggs, 2002).

Although there is a relatively large knowledge base on improving children's behavior through effective instruction and classroom management, SW-PBS research within the classroom is best characterized as emerging at this point. However, the studies conducted to date do show promise. For example, Langland, Lewis-Palmer, and Sugai (1998) found that application of universal supports was related to reductions in problem behaviors across two middle school classrooms. Stichter, Lewis, Johnson, and Trussell (2004) demonstrated improved behavior for a child with behavioral disorders in an elementary school classroom after the implementation of classroom-based PBS strategies (e.g., improving routines, clear expectations, and consistency). Stichter and Lewis (2005) also reported a clear relationship between the implementation of PBS strategies within the classroom and improved student behavior.

Abundant research has demonstrated the effectiveness of small-group/targeted supports such as social skill instruction, self-management, mentors, and academic assistance on social behavior. However, specifically within the context of SW-PBS, the benefit or additive impact of small-group strategies is emerging. For example, similar to the vast body of social skills research, Newcomer and Powers (2002) and Powers (2003)

demonstrated reductions in students' problem behavior following the implementation of small-group social skills programs. More important, both studies demonstrated that the teaching staff had a clear willingness to continue and to expand the program for additional students, two components typically lacking in the majority of social skills research conducted to date. Although universal and small-group/targeted interventions will be sufficient to support the majority of students, a small percentage will require more intensive individualized supports based on a functional behavioral assessment. Preliminary data show that interventions based on the function of problem behavior reduce problem behavior better than non-function-based interventions (Ingram, 2002; Newcomer & Lewis, 2004) and that individual plans are of higher quality if they are directly linked to universal SW-PBS systems (Newcomer & Lewis, 2004).

To date, there is much less research on the effectiveness of PW-PBS at the preschool level in comparison to elementary school settings. However, as with older children, related work to date is encouraging. For example, research conducted in a Head Start setting showed that young children who received a 12-week social skills intervention increased their adaptive behavior and decreased their problem behavior (Serna, Nielsen, Lambros, & Forness, 2000). Other research found that direct instruction of social skills and increases in the use of prompts and praise were associated with improved social outcomes (Stormont, Smith, & Lewis, in press; Tankersley, Kamps, Mancina, & Weidinger, 1996). Covington-Smith (2004) found that Head Start teachers who displayed low rates of universal PW-PBS essential features (e.g., prompts, verbal praise) were able to increase their usage with limited technical assistance. More important, the increased usage of PW-PBS skills had a dramatic impact on the rates of acting-out and aggressive behavior displayed by young children at high risk for behavioral disorders. The Covington-Smith findings are especially encouraging, and other research has also found that preschool teachers recognize the importance of consistent implementation of essential features of PW-PBS (Stormont, Lewis, & Covington, 2005) and, that after minimal professional development, most teachers will increase their use of key behavioral supports (Stormont, Covington, & Lewis, 2006).

SUMMARY

In order for school professionals to reduce problem behavior and develop healthy behavioral pathways for young children, it is essential that educators adopt effective, systemic behavior support strategies. This is especially important for educators of young children because early experiences often

lead to problem behavior in both preschool and elementary school. These early behavior patterns may then develop into chronic patterns of intense antisocial behavior if effective interventions are not put in place before Grade 3 (Walker et al., 2004). The key is building on the strength of the educator's craft: the ability to teach. The challenge is to ensure that all educators and school support personnel are fluent in teaching social skills. It is also important that schools and programs use data to guide the type and intensity of behavioral instruction and build systems of support to allow educators to implement strategies efficiently and effectively across the school year. PW/SW-PBS incorporates research-validated practices through a continuum of supports and embeds data-based decision making and systems to support educators, leading to significant reductions in problem behaviors.

TEXT OVERVIEW

Essential features of PW/SW-PBS systems are reviewed in detail in this text along with instruments to guide school/program implementation. In addition, numerous examples are provided to illustrate how schools and programs we have worked with have developed their own PW/SW-PBS systems based on the essential features. As you make your way through this text, it is important that you develop your own set of behavioral supports for each level of the continuum based on presenting behavioral concerns, available resources, and current research-based practices and not simply take the examples and attempt to implement them verbatim within your school or program. As stated previously, PW/SW-PBS is not a curriculum or ready-made discipline package. Research has clearly supported the principle that educators must build effective systems of prevention/early intervention that fit within and respond to their unique context (Gresham et al., 2001). Although all of the schools and programs we and our colleagues across the country work with have a common set of features, each is unique in what it teaches, variations in lessons, how it responds to students based on local norms and culture, and the focus of each level based on its unique set of behavioral challenges.

In addition to essential features that make up the "how-to," or critical, steps in developing PW/SW-PBS, several important themes and features throughout the text are critical to successful implementation. The first is an understanding of the overall process and system supports needed and the importance and role of the teams that drive the PW/SW-PBS process. These are expanded on in Chapters 2 and 3. Once the foundation for the overall process is presented, the key features are discussed in Chapters 4, 5, 6, and 7 and include the following:

- Teaching appropriate behavior (Chapter 4)
- Supporting appropriate behavior (Chapter 5)
- Using consequences (Chapter 6)
- Using data to make decisions (Chapter 7)

Finally, an overview of the small-group and individualized supports that can be used with children with more intense needs is presented in Chapter 8.

2 Supporting Systems Change

In Chapter 1, essential features for building programwide/schoolwide PBS (PW/SW-PBS) programs were overviewed. One of the most important features in implementing PW/SW-PBS is careful attention to the *systems* needed for successful implementation. Systems within the PW/SW-PBS process refer to training, technical assistance, and other supports the *adults* in the school environment need to implement and sustain best practices for students. Too often educators focus solely on what supports students need and make assumptions that their colleagues will have the skills, time, and necessary supports to implement practices without assistance. This assumption has resulted in the failure of many attempts at implementing best practices in schools. More than a decade ago, Kauffman (1993) eloquently stated the need for strong systems within schools: "Attempts to reform education will make little difference until reformers understand that schools must exist as much for teachers as for students. Put another way, schools will be successful in nurturing the intellectual, social, and moral development of children only to the extent that they also nurture such development of teachers" (p. 7).

Education has a long history of inservice professional development, which has helped to ensure that educators are up to speed with recent innovations as well as basic instructional and classroom management practices. Unfortunately, the vast majority of evaluative research on inservice efforts points to their failure to significantly change practices in school (Guskey, 2000). The issue is simultaneously simple and complex and mirrors the struggle to promote generalized responding among many of our students. At its most basic, the key to learning and behavior change is the simple fact that behavior is functionally related to the teaching environment. A functional relationship refers to the fact that behaviors occur predictably in the presence of some events, but not others, based on past learning experiences. Walk into a third-grade classroom and you will not hear students shouting out state capitals throughout the school day. However, while observing social studies in that same classroom, after the teacher asks, "What is the capital of Oregon?," you are likely to hear students respond "Salem." The behavior of stating "Salem" is functionally related to the prompt from the teacher, "What is the capital of Oregon?" (teaching environment). The teacher cannot "make" the students say Salem; she can simply provide the prompt. However, also based on past learning experiences, the children have learned that when they answer the question correctly, they are positively reinforced by, for example, good grades or teacher praise, another important component of the teaching environment. Through the sequence of teacher prompt (teaching environment), student correct response (behavior), and positive reinforcement (teaching environment), a functional relationship is developed, and we expect students to produce the behavior (in this case the correct capital) in the future and in other contexts, provided they are prompted to do so.

At their most complex, teaching environments are incredibly diverse settings made up of students and adults with varied backgrounds. The focus of PW/SW-PBS is on successful outcomes for all students, acknowledging that different individuals will need different levels of support (i.e., universals through individualized). However, it is important to keep in mind that, at the system level, school faculties are also made up of individuals who will need differing levels of support based on prior learning experiences. At the same time, the need for a continuum of supports firmly grounded in a consistent universal focus is also needed. The bottom line is that if schools are to successfully implement PW/SW-PBS, they must understand that behavior is functionally related to the teaching environment and build an environment that provides simultaneous support for students and adults. The common set of expectations and clear teaching and acknowledgment practices, as discussed in later chapters, are the basic "how-to" steps to develop a consistent and predictable teaching environment, thereby increasing the likelihood that students engage in appropriate behavior. In essence, children's appropriate social behavior becomes functionally related to the supported proactive teaching environments educators build through the PW/SW-PBS process.

It is important to emphasize that careful attention to constructing a proactive, supportive teaching environment for the adults within a school is also critical. In fact, without the appropriate adult environment, PW/SW-PBS will not be successful. Therefore, the remainder of this chapter focuses on how to build supportive systems at district, school, and program levels. First, the basic building blocks to construct a district/school/program system as recommended by the OSEP Center on Positive Behavioral Interventions and Supports are presented. Several pivotal features are then discussed.

CREATING A STATEWIDE, DISTRICTWIDE, OR PROGRAMWIDE SYSTEM

The OSEP Center on Positive Behavioral Interventions and Supports (2004) lists nine essential features for creating a systemic approach to SW-PBS at the state/district/program level (see Table 2.1). The key first essential feature is establishing a leadership team. Ideally, the leadership team is made up of representatives of the state/district/program. For example, a district team might have assistant superintendents that represent elementary and secondary schools, specialist directors such as special education or guidance counseling, curriculum coordinators, a professional development coordinator, two or three building principals, and two or three teachers. The goal is to make sure that several voices are heard in the planning process and that each team member is charged with effectively communicating the overall PW/SW-PBS plan to his or her representative constituents. The leadership team is responsible for the additional eight features for successful implementation. For example, specific tasks of the leadership team include (a) securing funding, (b) making PW/SW-PBS a priority, and (c) evaluating PW/SW-PBS efforts. One of the most important tasks of the leadership team is carefully planning professional development and ongoing technical assistance for school and program teams, both of which are described in more detail later. An additional key leadership team task is the appointment of a state/district/program-level coordinator. The coordinator is critical for success to ensure that detail within each step is carefully thought through, planned out, and implemented. Table 2.2 provides an overview of responsibilities of a state/district/program-level coordinator.

GETTING STARTED

States/districts/programs are often overwhelmed by the task of developing, implementing, and coordinating initiatives such as PW/SW-PBS because it is unlike other initiatives, which may easily fold into current systems or processes already in place. This is especially true when considering the scale of statewide implementation efforts or even implementation in large school districts. Unlike introducing a new textbook or scope and sequence within an academic subject that can often be addressed

Table 2.1 Essential System Features

Feature	Brief summary
Leadership team	Represents key stakeholders within the unit (e.g., state or district). Team develops an action plan and ensures necessary supports are in place, allowing districts/schools/classrooms to be successful.
Coordination	The leadership team designates person(s) to oversee the day-to-day operations of implementation.
Funding	Funding earmarked/identified by the leadership team to support, at minimum, three years
Visibility	Leadership team and coordinator effectively promote the PW/SW-PBS initiative within the state/district/program and local community to ensure understanding, and receive updates on progress.
Political support	PW/SW-PBS efforts become codified within existing state/district/program policies and procedures to underscore the priority within the state/district/program.
Training capacity	Trainers fluent with PW/SW-PBS available to train school/program teams, "PBS coaches," and other personnel within the state/district/program
Coaching capacity	Technical assistance is available at the school/program team level to assist with implementation.
Demonstrations	The state/district/program develops several schools/programs that are effectively implementing PW/SW-PBS to serve as exemplars.
Evaluation	Formative dynamic evaluation plan in place to determine impact of PW/SW-PBS, assess what can be done differently in instances where impact is not as great as expected, and plan for next steps

SOURCE Adapted from *School-Wide Positive Behavior Support: Implementers' Blueprint and Self-Assessment,* by OSEP Center on Positive Behavioral Interventions and Supports, 2004, Eugene, OR: Author.

Table 2.2   Schoolwide Positive Behavior Support District Coordinator: Sample Roles and Responsibilities

Professional Development

- Coordinate professional development opportunities for current teams

- Assist with training of new teams

- Coordinate coaches training

- Work with related centers, state departments, and districts that are implementing PW/SW-PBS on development of resource bank (e.g., materials, examples, updates of Web site)

Communication

- Coordinate communication across district

- Attend principal and assistant principal meetings to provide PW/SW-PBS updates and to listen to school concerns/questions

- Prepare quarterly and annual reports on progress of the district initiative for leadership team

- Develop district PW/SW-PBS handbook

Coordination

- Prepare leadership team agenda

- Maintain file of building meeting minutes, coach logs, and other data sources from school teams

- Meet with district coaches to problem solve

- Develop connections between PW/SW-PBS initiative and district school improvement plan

- Develop linkages to external agencies and PW/SW-PBS (e.g., mental health)

- Explore funding opportunities to expand and support initiative

SOURCE Adapted from Maryland PBIS, developed by the University of Missouri Center for School-wide Positive Behavior Support.

through an inservice and minimal follow-up model, PW/SW-PBS requires a fundamental shift in the way most schools approach discipline and requires true cross-school/program collaboration. An additional important difference is a shift from training and supporting individual teachers/classrooms to a focus on the program/school leadership team (see Chapter 3 for more information on establishing school teams).

The goal of PW/SW-PBS system support is to move away from a case-by-case approach using "experts" to address problems within schools. Instead, state/district/program efforts should focus on providing the training and technical assistance to allow PW/SW-PBS teams to solve their own problems, including more efficient use of specialists. In others words, instead of the state or district sending a behavior consultant to work with an individual teacher who has a difficult student, the consultant works with the school team to teach them how to assess the situation and build solutions based on gathered data. By shifting the focus of professional development and technical assistance to the school team, resources can be used more efficiently and school teams become fluent in both preventing future problems based on what they have learned and addressing problems that come up in a timelier manner. Put another way, schools rely less on outside experts and instead build expertise within their schools (Lewis & Newcomer, 2002). The following steps are offered as a starting point to begin this process.

Step 1: Form a leadership team with appropriate representatives from the state/district/program. Key first steps of the leadership team will be to establish (a) visibility in the state/district/program and community; (b) a clear statement of commitment to make PW/SW-PBS a top priority; (c) funding sources; (d) a state/district/program PBS coordinator; (e) the goals and outcomes of PW/SW-PBS mapped to state, district, or program goals and objectives; and (f) the development of a multiyear plan.

Step 2: Provide awareness sessions (e.g., one-hour overviews with a question-and-answer period) for state/district/program leadership, school principals, and a sample of teachers and parents.

Step 3: Establish a process for selection of initial school/program teams. Criteria for selection should minimally include selecting schools/programs with strong principal/administrator participation and selecting a cohort of schools/programs to establish exemplar schools/programs for the future. Therefore, schools in crisis should not be selected for the initial cohort. It is also important to determine the baseline data that will be obtained to monitor progress (e.g., suspensions, achievement).

Step 4: Establish a training schedule. Three parallel professional development activities should be targeted. The first is training for **PBS coaches**, who will provide within-state/district/program technical assistance to school teams. The second is for **school/program teams**. The third is laying the foundation to create a cohort of **within-state/district/program trainers.**

BUILDING CAPACITY AT THE SCHOOL/PROGRAM LEVEL

Keep in mind that the goal of all professional development and technical assistance is to build capacity at the school/program level. Capacity is defined as fluency in the three essential elements of PW/SW-PBS: (a) using data to make decisions, (b) adopting research-validated practices to support students, and (c) implementing systems to sustain effective practice use along a continuum of behavioral supports. In particular, careful attention must be paid to building effective systems to allow school teams to effectively implement needed practices. As stated in Step 4, capacity is built at the school/program level through three levels of professional development. The first feature is developing a cohort of trainers, or identifying existing experts in PW/SW-PBS, to train teams and coaches. The second is school/program team training in which the team learns the essential features of PW/SW-PBS and begins the action planning process. The third focuses on preparing PBS coaches to provide on-site technical assistance to school/program teams. Each of the three levels is described further in the next section.

PW/SW-PBS Trainers. The first level of professional development is to ensure that the other two levels of professional development are provided by personnel with expertise and experience with PW/SW-PBS. Initially, states/districts/programs rely on external trainers to begin the process and develop exemplar schools/programs. Throughout the process, coordinators, coaches, and team members gain sufficient fluency and experience to begin training their colleagues. Fortunately, resources are available, in many cases online, to assist states/districts/programs and include the OSEP Center on Positive Behavioral Interventions and Supports online library (www.pbis.org). Figure 2.1 provides minimum competencies for PW/SW-PBS trainers.

Figure 2.1 Coach, trainer, and coordinator competencies

Competency level	Skill mastery		
	Data	Practices	Systems
Level One (coaches):			
• Fluency at universal level • "Lead" teams through process (direct)	• Multiple data collection systems • Problem solving with data	• Schoolwide PBS essential features • Effective instruction • Classroom management • Rules to inform adoption of practices • Model school examples • Basics of ABA • PBS responses to problem behavior	• Meetings/team roles • Communication within building • Consultation • Targeted technical assistance • Task analysis of team generated universal practices for implementation • Codify practices into policy
Level Two (coaches/trainers):			
• Established effective school site(s) • Fluency at small-group and individual student level • Work with school team chair (indirect) • Train teams in universals	• Research data collection tools (e.g., SET) • Direct observation data at individual student level	• Advance ABA • Functional behavioral assessment • Social skill instruction	• Systematic (data-based) student identification for small-group/individual supports • Create/support student support team or process • Task analysis of team generated small-group/individual practices for implementation • Adapting universal systems to support generalization of small-group/individual plans • Consult with other agencies/parents • Codify practices into policy

Competency level	Skill mastery		
	Data	Practices	Systems
Level Three (coordinator):			
• Work with multiple schools • Train teams universal, individual level • Train coaches • Establish districtwide system	• Evaluation of districtwide efforts • Data decision rules to identify needed supports within/across schools • Link school needs (data-based) to district professional development	• Effective professional development/ training skills • Map district policy to essential features of PBS	• Leadership team roles/meetings • Communication across district • Resource bank ("experts" and materials) • Codify practices into policy

NOTES PBS = positive behavior support; ABA = applied behavior analysis; SET = schoolwide evaluation tool.

SOURCE Courtesy of the University of Missouri Center for School-wide PBS

School/Program Team Training. Training for schools/programs should provide the team with enough information to begin the process of developing universal supports. At a minimum, teams should be taught to

1. Assess current problems through multiple data sources.

2. Develop a common set of expectations to replace current problem behaviors.

3. Develop strategies to teach the school/programwide expectations.

4. Develop a system to acknowledge student mastery of skills.

5. Develop or refine a data collection and management system to inform practice.

6. Focus on building local capacity by attending to support needs of their colleagues.

Each of these components is described in detail with examples throughout this text. Once the school team consistently implements universal supports (Chapters 4, 5, and 6), training should focus on developing small-group and individual behavior support strategies along with data decision rules to identify students who need more supports and developing efficient systems to support faculty and staff (Chapters 7 and 8). Although educators often ask for a formula regarding the format, duration, and timing of the training, we recommend the state/district/program focus less on replicating format and more on developing positive outcomes. In other words, the program should provide training for teams in a manner that makes sense for the individual school/program but should also ensure that the outcome is team fluency and correct implementation according to assessments, such as those offered in this text, and through other SW-PBS resources.

PBS Coaches. It is also absolutely critical to the success of PW/SW-PBS implementation to develop a cadre of school/program staff who can provide on-site technical assistance. As this text will make clear, PW/SW-PBS is not a standard curriculum or set of practices. Although the thousands of schools implementing PW/SW-PBS follow a standard process (e.g., teaching expectations, building a connected continuum of supports), each adapts the process to respond to unique challenges as well as resource and community issues. Therefore, states/districts/programs should plan, especially during the initial stages of implementation, to provide on-site assistance. Most states/districts/programs accomplish this with existing personnel through the development of internal and external PBS coaches. An internal coach is a member of the school staff who has some job flexibility and/or whose current job is primarily to address behavioral issues. Examples of logical choices for internal coaches include assistant principals, guidance counselors, and resource special educators. External coaches are often school psychologists, behavior consultants, or other personnel with behavioral expertise who often serve several schools/classrooms. Remember: The critical difference with the latter is that the PW/SW-PBS process shifts their focus to working with teams, not just individual teachers or students. If funds allow, the ideal at any level—state, district, or program—is to hire full-time PBS coaches.

PBS coaches should have a firm grasp of the essential features of PW/SW-PBS and how to problem solve to ensure the team is moving down the right path (see Figure 2.1). Figure 2.2 provides a checklist of critical features to consider across the three elements of data, systems, and practices (see Figure 1.2) as well as the translation of work into policy. PBS coaches should keep the list in front of them each time they meet with the school team. Take, for example, something as simple as changing the routine during lunch time. First, the team should rely on proven practices, something the coach can assist with by sharing past research. Also critical in the selection of the new routine is ensuring "buy-in" from colleagues regarding the proposed practice. Each team member should present all proposed practices and procedures to their colleagues for feedback. By gaining feedback, the team is gaining buy-in and support. Once the practice or procedure is selected, the coach should prompt the series of questions under the systems component of the checklist. By prompting teams to answer simple logistical questions (e.g., When will teaching and cafeteria staff be trained on the new procedure? Who is going to do it?), the coach will get teams to consider system supports. Likewise, the coach should prompt team members to consider how they are going to measure impact (data) and encourage them to put new practice and procedures in writing (policy).

PBS coaches should also serve as facilitators between the school/program team and the state/district/program coordinator to share information. Coaches should let the coordinator know of professional development, technical assistance, or practice needs the team may have in order to provide timely support. Likewise, coaches should share available resources or professional development opportunities from the state/district. PBS coaches also typically assist with evaluation efforts, including how to address weaknesses. Effective professional development for PBS coaches should be monitored; however, the critical outcome will be competency in several skills.

Overall, PW/SW-PBS includes several professionals, with varying levels of expertise, to support implementation: coordinators assigned by an overarching leadership team, trainers, individual school/program teams, and PBS coaches. Figure 2.1 provides a list of competencies at each level of capacity building and should be used to guide skill development among PBS coaches, trainers, and the coordinator.

SUMMARY

The remainder of this text focuses primarily on the essential steps to implement PW/SW-PBS in preschool and elementary school settings. It is important to keep in mind that states/districts/programs should simultaneously develop the necessary system supports to build capacity across schools or program. Likewise, the supports offered at the state, district, or program level, including the coordinator, PBS coaches, and trainers, should focus on building capacity at the school or program level through the team. Capacity at the local level should include the necessary professional development and technical assistance to promote fluency with data, systems, and practices across the continuum. Capacity building, in particular, should focus on teaching school teams to develop systems of support within their schools or programs by focusing on what the *adults* will need to be successful. Failing to attend to systems or overlooking systems by making assumptions about what educators should know typically results in failure to impact student behavior, leading to understandable frustration on the part of the staff.

Figure 2.2 Schoolwide positive behavior support process analysis checklist

PBS feature	Critical components	In place	Plan to put in place
Practices (what we do for students)			
	Outcomes/objectives		
	Research supported		
	Technical assistance input		
	Stakeholder input		
Systems (how we support adults)			
	Evaluate current systems (develop new system or modify system)		
	Allocate/reallocate resources		
	Develop process/model and forms (adult and students)		
	Training		
	Information dissemination		
	Ongoing support (adult and students)		
	Develop formative evaluation process (student outcomes, adult use, success, and barriers)		
	Provide frequent positive and instructional feedback to staff		

PBS feature	Critical components	In place	Plan to put in place
Data (how we make decisions)			
	Student outcomes		
	Adult perceptions		
	System analyses		
	Cost–benefit		
Policy (how to maintain change)			
	Operationalize all processes		
	Codify within existing policy or create new policies		
	Dissemination to multiple audiences		

SOURCE Courtesy of the University of Missouri Center for School-wide PBS

3 Team Leadership

Team leadership in instituting programwide/schoolwide PBS (PW/SW-PBS) practices is an essential systems component; without teams, PBS efforts would not be effective. Teams apply the key principles and practices of PW/SW-PBS in a way that fits with the culture of their schools. As stated earlier, PW/SW-PBS is not a curriculum, and the team is responsible for determining where, when, how, and with whom the key features will be implemented. Teams also analyze progress using data as often as possible and from as many sources as possible. Thus, they are essential for both initiating and monitoring PW/SW-PBS efforts. Their work in the early years of implementation is extensive and ongoing. Then, even after the school and the team seem to work like a "well-oiled machine," they continue to use data to monitor efforts. Teams at every level of implementation are constantly working toward improving practices and strengthening systems to support staff and children. For example, teams in their first year of implementation may be focused on implementation efforts for all children by establishing universal behavioral expectations. Teams in their fifth year of implementation may be working toward establishing links with outside agencies in their communities to support individual children with severe behavior problems.

To guide implementation efforts, teams need to be cognizant of research-based practices related to school change and professional development. Research informs us that professional development should be intentional, ongoing, and systemic (Boudah, Logan, & Greenwood, 2001; Guskey, 2000). Chapter 2 provided information on the systemic efforts that need to be in place for PW/SW-PBS teams. The purpose of this chapter is to provide other pertinent information related to teams, including their formation, initial planning efforts, job assignments within teams, agendas, data collection efforts for monitoring progress, and professional development efforts.

FORMING A PW/SW-PBS TEAM

The person who initiates team formation varies. In some cases, principals may form or at least initiate the formation of teams. In other instances, a school psychologist or an early childhood behavioral consultant may initiate the process. When the PW/SW-PBS efforts are not instigated by an administrator, the administration still needs to provide support for the process. As discussed in Chapter 2, administrative support is a vital systems component (Boudah et al., 2001; Klinger, Ahwee, Pilonieta, & Menendez, 2003). Teams in elementary schools should include a group representative of the school. As such, the team should include the principal or assistant principal, a teacher for each grade level, a parent, and at least one professional with expertise in problem behavior. School psychologists, counselors, speech pathologists, and other staff should also be involved as resources permit. Individual schools should determine additional people who would be appropriate. For example, a physical education teacher who is respected immensely by staff and children would be a great person to communicate information to staff and support implementation efforts.

Forming early childhood teams is typically more complicated because early childhood programs are often spread across a school district and may include multiple types of classrooms. Several different programs may work together and share some of the same staff. For example, an early childhood special education program may also include a Title I program or a tuition-based preschool. In these cases, it is important that the team have members that represent all programs. Early childhood programs also include more related service providers, including occupational therapists, physical therapists, school psychologists, and speech pathologists. Ideally, a team will have one provider representing each related service in the program. Head Start programs include family advocates and "adopted grandmothers" for classrooms, and including representatives for these roles on PW-PBS teams is also important. Given that early childhood programs that serve at-risk children and children with identified disabilities have multiple professionals who are involved with children and staff, programwide teams can be very large and may include up to 20 professionals.

INITIAL PLANNING EFFORTS

As discussed in Chapter 2, training school teams in PW/SW-PBS is an important step in supporting the systemic piece of PBS. At the beginning stages, teams spend an extensive amount of time analyzing their school's or program's strengths and needs. A needs assessment is a critical part of this process (see Figure 3.1 for an example of a needs assessment for an early

Figure 3.1	Assessing behavioral support in early childhood settings

1. Name of school _____

2. Name and position of person completing this survey (**optional**)

_____

3. Number of students in your class/caseload _____

4. Estimate of number of students with chronic problem behaviors (i.e., those students who require extensive individualized support) _____

This survey was developed for use by early childhood teachers to assess the behavioral support strategies used in their classrooms and the level of available program support to assist them in supporting students with challenging behavior. The information from this survey can be used to assess what is in place, what works, and what needs to be modified. Please complete the following steps when completing the survey.

- When completing the survey teachers should do so independently.

- Teachers should first evaluate the degree to which each support is currently being implemented in their classrooms (i.e., *in place, partially in place, not in place*) on the **left-hand side of survey**.

- Next, teachers should evaluate the degree to which their program has provided or could currently provide support for each item on the **right-hand side of survey**.

Level of implementation			Feature	Available program support		
In place	*Partially in place*	*Not in place*		*In place*	*Partially in place*	*Not in place*
			1. Rules for the classroom are clearly defined.			
			2. Rules and expected student behaviors are taught directly in the classroom.			
			3. Rules and expected student behaviors are taught for nonclassroom settings such as the playground.			
			4. Continuum of procedures is in place to encourage child use of expected social behaviors.			

(Continued)

Figure 3.1 (Continued)

Level of implementation			Feature	Available program support		
In place	Partially in place	Not in place		In place	Partially in place	Not in place
			5. Procedures for encouraging expected behavior are implemented consistently by all staff.			
			6. A continuum of clear consequences exists for discouraging/ correcting problem behaviors.			
			7. Procedures for discouraging/ correcting problem behavior are implemented consistently by all staff.			
			8. Teachers have clear options that allow classroom instruction to continue when a student is disruptive.			
			9. Assistance from the preschool program is available to manage difficult student behavior during emergency or crisis situations.			
			10. Regular opportunities for teacher assistance for behavioral support in the classroom (e.g., observations, instructional strategies, coaching) are available from the preschool program.			

			11. Effective teaching practices are being used in the classroom (e.g., high rates of student engagement, students display high levels of accuracy with skills).			
			12. Effective preacademic curricula are being used in the classroom.			
			13. Developmental needs of individual students are accommodated.			
			14. Strategies are in place to identify students who do not respond to common behavior management strategies.			
			15. A range of small-group strategies is available to meet the needs of students with chronic problem behavior (e.g., social skills, self-management).			
			16. Someone with expertise to conduct functional behavioral assessments and design individualized support plans is available within or to the district (approx. 10 hours per week per student).			
			17. Significant family and/or community members are involved in individual student behavior plans when appropriate and possible.			

SOURCE Developed by University of Missouri Center for School-wide PBS; based on the Effective Behavior Support Survey developed by the OSEP Center on Positive Behavioral Interventions and Supports.

childhood program). When conducting a needs assessment, teams answer questions related to key features of PW/SW-PBS and their current level of implementation. Teams should also have a random sample of staff or all staff complete a needs assessment and use the data to inform planning.

It is vital that teams spend ample amounts of time determining their school's or program's needs and not rush to begin implementation. In the first year of implementation, teams should meet as often as possible, ideally on a weekly or biweekly basis. Teams have many different tasks related to getting PW/SW-PBS systems up and running, including

- Determining priorities and time frames.
- Assigning roles and running effective meetings.
- Determining data collection needs.
- Supporting professional development.
- Introducing PBS to children and families.

DETERMINING PRIORITIES AND TIME FRAMES

As stated previously, teams need to determine their school's or program's needs and plan accordingly. Teams may want to determine the changes that they want to see in three years and then create a three-year plan (R. Champion, personal communication, May 10, 2001). After three to five years, effective teams will have fully instituted all the key features presented in this book. However, some teams may choose to focus on implementing consistent consequences (Chapter 6) before teaching and supporting appropriate behavior (Chapters 4 and 5). Teams may also choose to focus on establishing universal behavioral expectations in Years 1 and 2 and wait until Year 3 to address the needs of children who need more support (Chapter 8). Alternatively, teams may spend an entire year meeting and planning and begin implementation the following year. Figure 3.2 is an example of how one elementary school implemented the key features of SW-PBS across a five-year time span.

With so many features to implement and systemic pieces to support, determining priorities helps teams begin implementation without becoming overwhelmed. Figure 3.3 is a summary of a needs assessment for an early childhood program. The summary articulates the strengths, needs, and areas of concern. This team held a meeting to discuss these results and agreed to make the need for a crisis plan for children with very challenging behavior a priority. To help determine priorities, in addition to the needs assessment related to key features of PBS, teams could also collect information from staff, children, and families. This could be done by

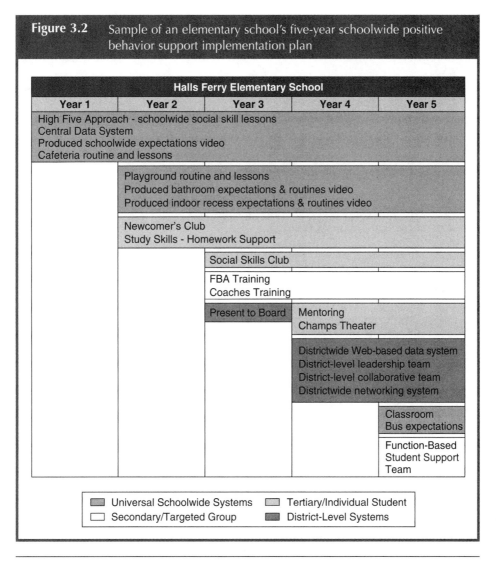

Figure 3.2 Sample of an elementary school's five-year schoolwide positive behavior support implementation plan

Halls Ferry Elementary School				
Year 1	**Year 2**	**Year 3**	**Year 4**	**Year 5**
High Five Approach - schoolwide social skill lessons Central Data System Produced schoolwide expectations video Cafeteria routine and lessons				
	Playground routine and lessons Produced bathroom expectations & routines video Produced indoor recess expectations & routines video			
	Newcomer's Club Study Skills - Homework Support			
		Social Skills Club		
		FBA Training Coaches Training		
		Present to Board	Mentoring Champs Theater	
			Districtwide Web-based data system District-level leadership team District-level collaborative team Districtwide networking system	
				Classroom Bus expectations
				Function-Based Student Support Team

▨ Universal Schoolwide Systems	☐ Tertiary/Individual Student
☐ Secondary/Targeted Group	▰ District-Level Systems

NOTE FBA = functional behavior assessment

creating and distributing a survey to a random sample of children, staff, and families or, if resources allow, to a larger representative group. Teams could also conduct interviews. If staff are involved in determining priorities, they are more likely to be motivated to learn the skills they need and be more engaged in professional development (Hawley & Valli, 1999). Once priorities are determined, teams need to create action plans and specific steps for addressing targets for change. Overall, teams need to remember to "think big but start small" (Missouri Positive Behavior Support Initiative, 2002, p. 18). Teams also need to work systematically to meet their goals, which includes assigning members to specific roles and using meeting time wisely.

Figure 3.3 Early childhood positive behavior support needs assessment summary

1. List the major strengths:
   a. Developmental needs of individual students are accommodated.
   b. Rules for the classroom are clearly defined.
   c. Effective teaching practices are being used in the classroom.

2. List major areas in need of development:
   a. Strategies are in place to identify students who do not respond to common behavior management strategies.
   b. A range of small-group strategies is available to meet the needs of students with chronic problem behavior.
   c. Procedures for discouraging/correcting problem behavior are implemented consistently by all staff.

3. Other areas of concern:
   a. A continuum of clear consequences for discouraging/correcting problem behavior is in place.
   b. A continuum of procedures is in place to encourage the child to use expected social behaviors.
   c. Procedures for encouraging expected behaviors are implemented consistently by all staff.
   d. Family members/community members are involved in individual student's behavior plans.

4. State the area in most need of development
   a. Assistance from the preschool program is available to manage difficult student behavior during emergency or crisis situations.

ASSIGNING ROLES AND RUNNING EFFECTIVE MEETINGS

It is important for PBS teams to be efficient and effective. As such, teams should assign members roles during meetings and roles to support their efforts between meetings. The most common roles and their responsibilities include the following:

- *Facilitator*—responsible for keeping conversations focused, positive, and constructive during team meetings. Also develops the meeting agenda and follows up with committees and tasks between meetings.
- *Recorder*—responsible for taking notes during meetings. Also responsible for distributing minutes to members.
- *Timekeeper*—responsible for keeping the team cognizant of the time allotted for discussing certain items. This person brings the group back to task and summarizes main points of meetings. The timekeeper and the facilitator keep the meeting focused and attempt to ensure that all agenda items are discussed.
- *Communication coordinator*—responsible for communicating back to staff, families, and children the results of PBS team meetings and the main priorities and goals for programs and schools at any given time. This person may also communicate successes to staff and provide staff with implementation exemplars. Communication efforts could consist of person-to-person contacts, displays on bulletin boards, notes in written newsletters, and presentations at school meetings. In larger schools and programs, there may be several communication coordinators.
- *Database manager*—responsible for inputting, analyzing, and presenting data to the team. This person should be very familiar with data management programs, such as Excel, and should be willing to spend the time needed to manage data. Chapter 7 further discusses the role of the database manager.

Teams may assign other roles and responsibilities, including a team "cheerleader" or an archivist (Figure 3.4).

Another way to promote efficient meetings is to have a structured meeting agenda to facilitate timeliness and clarity of assignments. Figures 3.5 and 3.6 are templates that can be used to promote efficiency in meetings. Using templates would certainly support the facilitator, timekeeper, and recorder by having a consistent overall structure to frame meetings, time allotted for specific topics, and the outline already established before the meetings. The table at the bottom of Figure 3.5 also adds support for the facilitator, who follows up on assignments between meetings. The "parking lot" section at the end of Figure 3.6 is a great way to acknowledge innovative ideas or the need to discuss something further in the future while keeping the team focused on the meeting agenda items (Zentall, 2006).

Figure 3.4	Positive behavior support team roles and responsibilities

Role	Responsibilities
Chairperson/facilitator	• Develop agenda • Facilitate meeting • Follow up on assigned tasks • Seek input from staff and other committees
Recorder/secretary	• Keep minutes • Distribute minutes to team members • Notify/remind team members of meeting time and location
Database manager	• Summarize data from previous month • Present update on standard data (e.g., office referrals) • Summarize data necessary for any pending decisions (e.g., effectiveness of new cafeteria routines)
Communication coordinator	• Report progress and data-based feedback to staff • Create/maintain newsletters, bulletins, teachers' lounge bulletin board • Maintain systems of communication with staff • Post expectations
Timekeeper/task master	• Monitor agenda times and topics • Keep the group focused and moving • Monitor start and end times • Table a subject or make a decision
Team cheerleader	• Monthly booster notes/treats for staff members • Plan staff celebrations and recognitions • Challenge staff to recognize efforts that support PBS process (putting notes of recognition in staff members' boxes)
Team archivist	• Maintain a database of team products (e.g., systems tools, forms, data collection forms) and back up database regularly • Make updates or edits to products and disseminate • Create an electronic archive for easy staff access to PBS team documents

SOURCE Developed by University of Missouri Center for School-wide Positive Behavior Support.

Figure 3.5   Sample early childhood positive behavior support (PBS) team meeting template

PBS Team Meeting Agenda

TEAM: _____ DATE: _____

EF	Task	Who reports	Time
Commitment			
Communication			
Team			
Define			
Teach			
Perform Feedback			
Response to Violations			
Data			
Tasks to work on this coming month		Who	Timeline

SOURCE Developed by University of Missouri Center for School-wide Positive Behavior Support.

Figure 3.6   Two sample elementary positive behavior support (PBS) team meeting templates

Template 1: PBS Team Meeting Agenda

TEAM: _____ DATE: _____

| PBS TEAM GOALS and NORMS | 1 minute |
| CELEBRATIONS! | 4 minutes |

			Task	Who reports	Time
Essential Features		Commitment			
		Communication			
		Team			
		Define			
		Teach			
	Perform Feedback				
	Response to Violations				
		Data			

| **SUMMARY of MEETING MAIN POINTS** | **2 minutes** |

Template 2: PBS Team Meeting Agenda for

<INSERT YOUR SCHOOL NAME HERE!>

Tasks to work on this coming month	Who	Timeline
A. Reporting out to team on the following points:	Team members	THIS WEEK!
1.		
2.		
3.		
4.		
B.		
C.		
D.		

"PARKING LOT" for GREAT IDEAS!

1.

2.

3.

4.

5.

DETERMINING DATA COLLECTION NEEDS

After teams have initiated PW/SW-PBS, teams need to monitor their school's or program's progress. The overall process that should guide data collection, types of data that can be collected, and use of data for decision making are discussed in depth in Chapter 7.

PROFESSIONAL DEVELOPMENT

For PW/SW-PBS to be effective, adult behavior must change. Professional development researchers have indicated that a "critical mass" of teachers must participate for efforts to be successful (Boudah et al., 2001). More specifically, experts in the change process suggest that 75% of teachers need to be on board in order for schoolwide or programwide efforts to be successful (Missouri Positive Behavior Support Initiative, 2002). This is quite a daunting task. With any school- or programwide systems change, one of the most important tasks for administration and teams driving the change process is to create a culture to support change. Professional development is a critical piece to supporting such a culture.

As discussed earlier, it typically takes three to five years to fully implement PW/SW-PBS. Professional development efforts in each of these years will vary according to where the school or program is in the change process. According to research in the area of professional development, change occurs in four phases (Missouri Positive Behavior Support Initiative, 2002):

1. Awareness.

2. Initial implementation and skill building.

3. Full implementation.

4. Skills and practice institutionalization.

Across these phases, professional development (PD) needs to be continual and driven by the desired outcomes. According to Hawley and Valli (1999), "Professional development should be driven by analyses of the differences between goals and standards for student learning and how students perform. Such analyses will define what educators need—rather than want—to learn, make professional development student centered, and increase public confidence in the use of resources for professional development" (as cited by Missouri Positive Behavior Support Initiative, 2002, p. 17). Although professional development needs to be anchored to desired outcomes among children, staff do need to have choices in how they are provided support for learning key features of PW/SW-PBS. Such choices (Boudah et al., 2001; Missouri Positive Behavior Support Initiative, 2002; Turnbull, Turnbull, Erwin, & Soodak, 2006) could include:

- Large-group presentations and trainings using a variety of formats according to learners' needs (e.g., lecture, discussion, seminar, role-play).
- Peer coaching, in which peers observe each other and provide feedback. This coaching could be anchored to specific goals for professional development (PD), including, for example, increasing teachers' use of precorrection and behavior-specific praise. Experts in PW/SW-PBS, such as trainers, could also serve as coaches. Coaches could use a checklist of universals to target specific needs for support (Figure 3.7).
- Mentors assigned to colleagues to provide support in the change process. Mentors could be either master teachers who are committed to PW/SW-PBS principles or PBS team members.
- Individual professional development goals and plans for improvement, which could then become part of a staff member's annual evaluation. Staff could target areas linked to PW/SW-PBS, determine how they will collect data on their performance, and identify resources they will need to promote their own professional development.

Evaluating professional development efforts is essential for determining whether efforts are leading to desired outcomes. To effectively evaluate PD, according to R. Champion (personal communication, May 10, 2001), teams should:

- Have a clear vision of the expected outcomes for different PD activities (e.g., awareness).
- Determine the data that will be gathered to evaluate PD when planning PD activities.
- Use objective and subjective data sources for a more complete picture of the impact of PD on adults and children.
- Make results from evaluation public.
- Keep everyone informed about how data are being used to improve PD.

As with students, some teachers and other staff will struggle and need more support in using key features. Providing more support and practice for these individuals is very important. As mentioned, mentors, coaching, and PD could be used to support struggling staff (Boudah et al., 2001).

Figure 3.7 Sample classroom universals inventory

Classroom: _____ Date: _____ Time: _____

Observer: _____ Purpose/focus: _____

Rate each feature using the following scale: 1 = inconsistent or unpredictable; 5 = consistent and predictable	1	2	3	4	5
I. Physical Space: Is physical space organized to allow access to instructional materials?					
• Work centers are easily identified and correspond with instruction.	1	2	3	4	5
• Traffic flow minimizes physical contact between peers and maximizes teacher's mobility.	1	2	3	4	5
II. Gain/Maintain Student Attention: Does the teacher gain the attention of the students prior to instruction?					
• A consistent and clear attention signal is used across instructional contexts.	1	2	3	4	5
• Teacher uses a variety of techniques to gain, maintain, and regain student attention to task.	1	2	3	4	5
III. Use of Time: Does the teacher initiate instructional cues and materials to gain, maintain, and regain student attention?					
• Materials are prepared and ready to go.	1	2	3	4	5
• Precorrects are given prior to transitions.	1	2	3	4	5
• Common intrusions are anticipated and handled with a consistent procedure. Unexpected intrusions are minimized with an emphasis on returning to instruction.	1	2	3	4	5
• Students engaged at high rates during individual work.	1	2	3	4	5
• Downtime (including transitions) is minimal.	1	2	3	4	5
IV. Behavior Management: Does the teacher have universal systems of PBS in place?					
• Rules are posted.	1	2	3	4	5
• Rules are referred to at appropriate times.	1	2	3	4	5
• Students receive verbal praise for following rules.	1	2	3	4	5
• Maintains a 4:1 ratio of positive to negative statements.	1	2	3	4	5
• Continuum for encouraging expected behaviors is used.	1	2	3	4	5
• Active supervision techniques (moving, scanning) are used throughout instruction.	1	2	3	4	5
• Corrections are made by restating the rule/expectation and stating the appropriate replacement behavior.	1	2	3	4	5
• Continuum of consequences for discouraging undesired behaviors.	1	2	3	4	5
V. Use of Routines: Does the teacher have procedures and routines that are clear and consistently followed?					
• Start of class.	1	2	3	4	5
• Working in groups.	1	2	3	4	5

• Working independently.	1	2	3	4	5
• Special events (movies, assemblies, snacks, parties).	1	2	3	4	5
• Obtaining materials and supplies.	1	2	3	4	5
• Using equipment (e.g., computer, tape players).	1	2	3	4	5
• Managing homework and other assignments.	1	2	3	4	5
• Personal belongings (e.g., coats, hats, backpacks).	1	2	3	4	5
• Entering/exiting classroom (e.g., using restroom/drinking fountain, going to library, during classroom instructional time).	1	2	3	4	5
VI. Curriculum, Content, & Delivery: Does the teacher implement effective instruction strategies?					
• Advanced organizer is used to set the stage for lesson (ties new instruction to past instruction, previews topic to be covered).	1	2	3	4	5
• Content is presented at student level, resulting in high rates of engagement.	1	2	3	4	5
• Frequently checks student learning for understanding.	1	2	3	4	5
• Instructional focus builds on student's current and past skills.	1	2	3	4	5
• Frequent opportunities to respond with academic accuracy are provided.	1	2	3	4	5
• Wait time is provided following prompts.	1	2	3	4	5
• Assignments can be completed within allotted time period.	1	2	3	4	5
• Gives clear set-up and directions for task completion.	1	2	3	4	5
• Follow-up steps (e.g., homework) are discussed.	1	2	3	4	5
• Mental or hard copy notes taken on how many students met the learning objective.	1	2	3	4	5
• Follow-up instructions for those who did not meet the objective are planned.	1	2	3	4	5
• Plans for what to do next time with this activity are made.	1	2	3	4	5

Based on the observation, summarize strengths and opportunities for improvement of the implementation of PBS classroom universals.

Areas	Opportunities for improvement (Scores 1–3)	Strengths (Scores 4–5)
Use of physical space		
Gain/maintain student attention		
Use of time		
Behavior management		
Use of routines		
Curriculum, content, and delivery		

SOURCE Adapted from OSEP Center on Positive Behavioral Interventions and Supports, 2004; Sugai & Tindal, 1993; Platt, Tripp, Ogden, & Fraser, 2000; developed by the University of Missouri Center for School-wide PBS.

Because the traditional reactive approach for working with social behavior is so different from PW/SW-PBS, it should be expected that some staff will have difficulty implementing these new practices. Accordingly, teams should have plans in place and multiple options to provide support for staff who are struggling. An example follows.

Mr. Miller Learns Precorrection

The PBS team at Park Elementary looks at office referral data (ODR) from second-grade teachers. Over a two-month period, the second-grade children, overall, have twice as many ODRs as any other grade. On closer examination, it is clear that one teacher is responsible for this difference across grades. As a result, the team decides to send the PBS trainer from their school to observe Mr. Miller. The trainer tells Mr. Miller that she is coming to provide support given the high number of ODRs he is reporting. Across one week, the trainer comes in three times. She notices a theme. Mr. Miller does not provide cues and prompts to get children ready for different setting expectations (precorrection), and he uses a lot of redirection and reprimands. She observes this in a transition context, during literacy time, and during small-group sharing. She meets with him to discuss her observations, and Mr. Miller and the trainer set a goal for an increase in precorrective prompts and cues. The two also practice what these may look like across different settings. The trainer asks Mr. Miller whether he would like her to model prompts and cues in different contexts the next week or whether Mr. Miller would like to observe another second-grade teacher who uses a lot of precorrective statements. Mr. Miller likes the idea of having the trainer model in his classroom the next week, and they set some times and settings for the trainer to model the target behaviors.

Another way to support teacher change is by helping teachers see the impact of their new practices on children's behavior (Boudah et al., 2001). In fact, research has found that one of the most common reasons teachers reported for sustaining use of research-based practices is seeing a connection between the practice and children's learning (Klinger, Arguelles, Hughes, & Vaughn, 2001). Although anticipating that children will benefit from a practice is also a motivating factor many teachers report for learning and using a practice, for others it is clear that this may need to occur before they are completely sold on the practice. Thus, professional development efforts with some struggling staff may include data collection on children (e.g., direct observation or ODRs) *after* teachers begin using key features with integrity. Over time, it is hoped that teachers will feel more empowered to solve problems in their classroom once they know how to pose problems, target solutions, and collect data on children's behavior (Boudah et al., 2001).

One early childhood program has another type of support for teachers to remind them of what setting factors they need to have in place to support children's behavior before a referral for special education is initiated. Figure 3.8 includes a list of questions that teachers have to complete for children they believe need extra support. This is not intended to be "red tape" in the referral process but rather a reflective activity for teachers. When completing this form, teachers need to consider their classroom rules, how they have taught them, when they have reviewed them, and how they have used precorrection and consequences.

PROMOTING PW/SW-PBS TO STAFF AND FAMILIES

Another responsibility of the PW/SW-PBS team is to promote the principles and practices to the staff, families, and children. The team may have several goals related to promoting an understanding of PW/SW-PBS in the first year of implementation. Teams may find promoting this system of supports to be easy or challenging, depending, in part, on the culture of the school or program. For example, it may be difficult to promote PW-PBS in a program that is beginning a new approach to curriculum and instruction at the same time. In other cases, teachers may have an overriding philosophy against using structure to support appropriate behavior (Boudah et al., 2001). In such instances, teachers must be supported in understanding how the principles and practices of PW/SW-PBS can fit within their belief systems regarding children's learning and development.

To support these efforts, teams can designate one person or several people to be vehicles for communication. The specific communication practices could include any of the following:

- Letters home to parents introducing PW/SW-PBS and specific practices that are being implemented
- Posters in schools and classrooms with pictures and/or words representing key principles and practices
- Meeting with parents on Parent-Teacher Organization nights or having a family night where PW/SW-PBS is discussed
- Having PW/SW-PBS updates and question-and-answer sessions as a standard agenda item at staff meetings

Figure 3.8 Sample request for behavioral consultant support

REQUEST FOR SOCIAL/EMOTIONAL/BEHAVIORAL SUPPORT

If you have referred someone from your classroom in the past six months and completed this page at that time, make note here in whose file we will find that information and do not complete this page.

_____

List your classroom rules:

_____   _____

_____   _____

_____   _____

How have the children been informed of these rules?

_____

_____

When/how often do you review the rules with the children?

_____

How have other adults in your environment been informed of these rules (aides, specialists, substitutes)?

_____

_____

Give examples of consequences for specific behavior you use in your classroom:

_____

_____

_____

_____

Give examples of how you inform children of behavior expectations for specific activities (precorrection):

_____

_____

_____

_____

Have you/another staff member completed behavior observations of this child in the school environment?_____ (Include copies of these observation sheets and/or charts.)

Parent involvement/conferences held concerning the behavior (include copies of conferences summaries):

_____

_____

_____

Date of parent contact concerning this referral: _____ Parent comments: _____

_____

_____

Parent[s] names: _____

Parent phone numbers: Home _____ Work: _____

Address: _____

_____

If you have any questions regarding this form, please contact _____

Please forward the following forms to: ____Request for S / E / B Support

_____   ____Release of information

Early childhood behavioral consultant   ____Parent/teacher conference summary

Early childhood special education   ____Copies of incident reports

                                              ____Copies of behavioral Observations/charts

                                              ____Daily schedule times

• Developing newsletters and fact sheets with case examples, hot topics, and common questions and answers and distributing them in teachers' lounges

Figure 3.9 is an example of a letter one early childhood program sent home to families that explains that the program is going to begin to emphasize two key features: collecting data on children's behavior through incident reports and teaching appropriate social behavior. In all communications, it is important to have one or two representatives from the PW/SW-PBS team who are available to answer questions and discuss any concerns.

Figure 3.9   Sample letter to parents regarding programwide positive behavior support topics

Early Childhood Positive Behavior Support

Parents,

_____ continues to develop an early childhood programwide positive behavior support system, which is a proactive early intervention program designed to teach social skills to preschoolers and to prevent and address challenging behavior in the schools.

One component of this program is the attached Behavior Incident Report. A major purpose of the report is to collect data. This will allow us to focus on interventions and strategies that may be necessary in your child's classroom. Parents will receive copies of the report as incidences occur. Minor concerns will, of course, be addressed by the teaching staff. You will notice the incident number at the top of the form. This will allow us to keep track of specific children who are having behavior difficulties and will give us information for creating plans to support their success.

A second element of positive behavior support is an ongoing, regular focus on preschool social skills. Each classroom will concentrate on the following themes during the school year through play, stories, games, role-playing, and other activities: Making Friends, Following Rules, Conflict Resolution, Feelings, Getting Along With Others, Self-Esteem, and Classroom Skills. You will receive information from your teacher about each set of lessons.

Please feel free to talk to you child's teacher or to call the Early Childhood Behavior Consultants (_____) with any questions or comments. We welcome your feedback!

Sincerely,

The Early Childhood Positive Behavior Support Team

SUMMARY

The gap between education research and practice is due, in part, to a lack of fit between research-based practice and the school context (Greenwood & Abbott, 2001). It is clear that implementing new practices based on research requires effort and time. The practice of having teams drive the PW/SW-PBS implementation efforts is an attempt to promote consistent use of research-based practices. It is up to the team to initiate and monitor efforts in a systematic fashion and to consider the culture of their individual schools and programs every step of the way. Teams are responsible for developing structures for each one of the key features of PW/SW-PBS presented in the remainder of this text.

4 Teach Behavioral Expectations

All children in schools and programs using programwide/schoolwide positive behavior support (PW/SW-PBS) are taught appropriate behavior. Again, this proactive orientation is often a stark contrast to the typical reactive approaches that schools have used and many continue to use for discouraging problem behavior (Sugai et al., 2000; Walker et al., 2004). This reactive orientation has been so widely accepted because children are often expected to come to school already possessing the social skills needed to be successful in school (Stormont, Beckner, Mitchell, & Richter, 2005). Children who do not have these social skills already in their repertoire may be expected to learn these skills with very little support or explicit instruction. Thus, children are told to be kind to friends but may not have a context for connecting specific social concepts (being kind to friends) to specific social behaviors (taking turns with materials, using nice words). Furthermore, some children's past experiences or learning histories have reinforced their use of negative social behavior (e.g., tantrums, aggression, whining). Traditionally, on school entry, children are expected to abandon these inappropriate social skills but receive little instruction and support for learning what to do instead. As addressed in Chapter 1, historically schools have not provided the same support for social development that they have for academic development.

Alternatively, in schools and programs implementing PW/SW-PBS, children are not expected to have certain preexisting social skills intact when they enter school or to learn social skills independently. The establishment of universal support strategies to prevent problem behavior while promoting appropriate behavior is the foundation for PW/SW-PBS. One universal support strategy includes establishing universal behavioral expectations for programs or schools. All children are then taught specific social behaviors that are expected across various settings throughout the school day. The expected or desired social skills are taught within the context of the school's or program's behavioral expectations. This chapter discusses the process by which behavioral expectations are chosen and specific behaviors are taught. Examples for preschool and elementary programs are infused throughout.

CHOOSE BEHAVIORAL EXPECTATIONS

One of the first tasks for teams implementing systems of PW/SW-PBS is to select their behavioral expectations. Behavioral expectations are the terms used to organize the specific social behaviors that are desired or expected in different settings across the school day. For example, one behavioral expectation may be "Be respectful," which is used to describe all social behaviors across the school day that represent respect. Respectful behaviors can include

- Using a calm tone of voice
- Saying "please" and "thank you"
- Listening to directions
- Listening while others are talking
- Sharing
- Waiting in line
- Helping friends
- Helping the teacher

Elementary schools should choose no more than six positively stated behavioral expectations for their students. In their selection process, teams typically review behavioral expectations that other schools have adopted and then determine how to individualize the expectations for their own schools. It is important that teams solicit staff input and try to support the creation of a set of expectations that represent the unique culture of their school or early childhood program. Figure 4.1 includes examples of behavioral expectations from different elementary programs.

Preschool programs implementing PW-PBS should select fewer expectations (three or less) and choose words that are developmentally appropriate for younger children (Stormont, Lewis, & Beckner, 2005). One preschool program implementing PW-PBS selected a single expectation: "Take care of ourselves, our friends, and our school." Other preschool programs have selected "Be safe, be kind, and be responsible" as the

---

Figure 4.1   Sample behavioral expectations

Be Safe
Be Respectful
Be Learners

High Five Expectations:

Be Kind
Be Safe
Be Peaceful
Be Responsible
Be Respectful

 *STARR Student Pledge:*

I am **S**afe.
I **T**ry hard.
I **A**chieve.
I am **R**espectful.
I am **R**esponsible.
I am, and always will be, a **STARR!**

---

behavioral expectations for their programs (Stormont, Lewis, & Beckner, 2005). "Be kind" is an expectation that can include the same types of behaviors that "respect" represents for older children. "Be safe" is also easy for young children to understand, because many behaviors that are stressed in early years are related to safety. Many preschool programs have chosen to emphasize "Be safe" and "Be kind" with their children and teach behaviors related to "Be responsible" as children get closer to their transition to kindergarten.

To support their transition to kindergarten, preschool programs should also consider whether their children are transitioning to elementary programs that are implementing SW-PBS. When applicable, to support their children's transition, preschool programs may want to select expectations that are used in certain elementary schools in their district. In the previous example, the preschool program chose "Be responsible" because it was one of the expectations for an elementary school that many children would be attending.

DETERMINE BEHAVIORS THAT REPRESENT EXPECTATIONS

After teams have selected their behavioral expectations, they need to determine what behaviors represent these expectations across settings. The process for determining the expectations and the specific rules or behaviors they represent is a critical one and begins with thinking about what appropriate behavior looks like in different settings. Often it is easier for professionals to determine what they do not want children to be doing in different settings (arguing, hitting, running), which can begin the process of focusing attention on what a replacement behavior would look like. The overall process for determining the behaviors that need to be targeted for instruction includes

- Determining problem behavior across different settings.
- Determining what children should do *instead* of the problem behavior across different settings. These specific behaviors represent the desired *replacement* behaviors (the rules or routines that need to be taught).
- Being *explicit in teaching* the desired replacement behavior. Social skills instruction and promotion are essential.

When using this process to determine instructional needs, the focus of behavior management shifts from reacting to problem behavior to focusing on what children should do instead. Accordingly, professionals need to determine specific behaviors that represent the expectations across the school day. Multiple settings need to be analyzed for current problem behaviors and the desired replacement behaviors, which become the target for instruction. For elementary schools, common settings include

- Classroom
- Cafeteria
- Playground
- Bathroom
- Hallway
- Gymnasium
- Office
- Bus

Several of these settings (e.g., office, hallway, gym) may be included in an "all school settings" category depending on the similarity of expected behaviors in such settings. Schools may also have other settings they need to add because they occur often, such as assemblies. Teachers can also individualize behavioral expectations in their classrooms by adding to the common core. However, the nonclassroom setting expectations should be established by the team, with staff input, and supported across all program/school settings. This common focus is important in that it provides the basic framework for universal supports that have been developed to reflect the unique culture of each program/school.

For preschool programs, common settings include classroom, playground, hallway, gymnasium, visitor, naptime, bus, and bathroom. Children in preschool classrooms typically eat in their rooms, nap in their rooms, and may leave their classroom only to go to the playground. However, specific settings can be connected to different points in time in the classroom, including naptime, lunchtime, or when a visitor is present. Further, even though children may not leave their classroom to go to the bathroom, there are different behaviors that can be taught and supported regarding bathroom behavior.

DEVELOP MATRIX TO SUPPORT COMMON LANGUAGE

After or while determining replacement behaviors for each setting, teams should create a matrix of all of the desired behaviors that represent the expectations across the school day. Matrices are tables with the specific settings listed horizontally across the top row and the behavioral expectations listed vertically in the far left-hand column. The team should create a draft matrix, circulate the draft among all staff in the program/school for feedback, and work toward creating a final version that reflects consensus to guide all related teaching and support activities in the program/school. These behaviors are considered to be teachable examples of what it looks like to "be safe" or to "be kind" in that setting. Staff should not attempt to place every appropriate behavior in each box; they should focus on the most important replacement behaviors for that setting based on current and common problem behaviors. Figures 4.2, 4.3, and 4.4 are examples of matrices developed by preschool and elementary programs.

Figure 4.2 Programwide expectations for an early childhood program

	Classroom	Bathroom	Playground
Be Safe	• Keep feet on ground • Use walking feet • Use inside voices	• Wash hands with soap and water • One person in a stall	• Go down slide on bottom • Rocks and wood chips stay on the ground
Be Kind	• Be a friend • Share with others • Use listening ears • Take care of our school	• Use inside voice • Keep hands to self	• Let others play • Keep body to self • Share with others • Use nice words
Be Responsible	• Be a good helper • Follow directions • Clean up • Make good choices	• Flush toilet • Turn off water • Clean up	• Use equipment correctly • Use line basics • Clean up

	Mealtime	Walkways	Bus/Van
Be Safe	• Push chairs in • Keep body to self	• Use walking feet • Stay with an adult	• Keep seatbelts on • Keep back to seat
Be Kind	• Use manners • Ask to be excused	• Use inside voice • Keep hands to self	• Use inside voice • Keep body to self
Be Responsible	• Keep food on plate • Clean up	• Use listening ears • Use line basics	• Listen to driver/monitor • Take care of own things • Follow bus rules

SOURCE Developed in collaboration with the University of Missouri Center for School-wide Positive Behavior Support.

Figure 4.3   Programwide matrix for an early childhood program

Setting →

Expectation ↓	Classroom	Bus	Hallway	Outside
Be Safe	• Use walking feet • Sit on our spots at circle • Pretzel legs at circle	• Sit in our seats • Listen to the driver • Wait on the sidewalk	• Use walking feet • Hands at our sides • Keep eyes forward	• Listen to the teachers • Slide on our bottoms • Watch out when driving tricycles
Be Kind	• Share toys • Quiet hands with friends • Use kind words with friends	• Say "Hi" to the bus driver	• Use quiet voices • Smile at friends we meet	• We can take turns on the slide and swings • We can use kind words
Be Responsible	• We can bring our books to school • Clean up • Wash our hands	• Remember our backpacks when we leave the bus	• Use quiet voices • Stay in our line	• Touch the fence when we hear the bell

SOURCE Developed in collaboration with the University of Missouri Center for School-wide Positive Behavior Support.

TEACH EACH SOCIAL BEHAVIOR

Professionals implementing PW/SW-PBS need to use a direct or explicit instruction approach to teach specific replacement behaviors that represent the behavioral expectations. For example, programs/schools would design a lesson to teach the classroom behavior "Follow teacher instructions the first time asked," which is listed on their matrix under "Be responsible" and "Classroom." Each specific behavior listed on the matrix needs to have a corresponding lesson to teach the behavior. The research base supporting the need for explicit instruction of social skills is extensive (e.g., Kauffman, 2005; Lewis, Powers, Kelk, & Newcomer, 2002; Scott, 2001; Serna et al., 2000; Walker et al., 2004).

Figure 4.4 Schoolwide expectations for an elementary school

Expectations	Settings								
	All settings	Hallways	Cafeteria	Restrooms	Playground/outdoor behavior	Walker	Car rider	Assemblies	Bus
Safe	Walk in building. Use materials and equipment appropriately. Chewing gum and candy should be left at home.	Watch where you are going.	Keep food on your tray. Push in chairs.	Wash hands with soap and water. Use facilities appropriately. Keep water in sink.	Use equipment appropriately. Stay in designated areas. Wood chips stay on the ground. Participate in school-approved games.	Do not accept rides from strangers. Walk directly to school/directly home. Stay on sidewalks. Cross street at designated areas.	Load/unload on the passenger side. Ask an adult before leaving area. Buckle your seat belt in the car.	Enter and exit the room in an orderly manner.	Remain seated while bus is moving. Cross in front of the bus. Stay out of street while waiting for bus.
A team player	Include others. Use polite words. Keep hands and feet to self. Help others. Be a friend.	Greet others with a smile.	Wait in line in order. Allow everyone to sit and eat.	Allow for privacy.	Invite others to join in. Include all who want to play. Accept skill differences.	Allow others to walk with you.	Greet others positively.	Listen to the presenter(s). Clap only when they are finished.	Allow others to sit with you. Greet driver with a smile.

| Expectations | Settings | | | | | | | | |
	All settings	Hallways	Cafeteria	Restrooms	Playground/ outdoor behavior	Walker	Car rider	Assemblies	Bus
A learner	Follow adult directions the first time. Take turns. Share with others. Problem solve. Be a team player. Use appropriate voice levels. Be a good listener.	Follow rules without reminders. Follow transition routines.	Sit at assigned spot. Wait for dismissal. Enter PIN and hand money to cashier.	Give turns. Follow bathroom procedures.	Agree on rules before starting. Follow game rules.	Listen/follow crossing guard directions.	Wait in a patient, orderly manner.	Raise hand to ask or answer questions if appropriate.	Wait your turn to exit. Keep your place in line. Wait quietly and patiently for your bus. Follow bus rules.
Respectful	Treat others the way you want to be treated. Allow others to be different. Acknowledge other's ideas.	Walk quietly so others can continue learning. Keep hands at your side and away from walls.	Eat only your food. Keep area clean. Use good manners.	Respect privacy of others. Clean up after self.	Keep the rules the same during the game. Use appropriate language (no put-downs).	Respect the property of homeowners.	Interact with courtesy to peers and adults.	Keep hands and feet to self. Stay seated in designated areas.	Keep it clean.

(Continued)

Figure 4.4 (Continued)

Expectations	Settings								
	All settings	Hallways	Cafeteria	Restrooms	Playground/ outdoor behavior	Walker	Car rider	Assemblies	Bus
	Honor other's personal space. Show positive body language.				Line up quietly when the whistle blows.				
Responsible	Take care of self. Do your job. Accept outcomes of behaviors. Make good choices. Be honest. Report problems to an adult. Allow others to resolve their own conflicts. Leave electronic devices and toys at home.	Make your way promptly to destinations.	Clean up after self. Make healthy choices. Remember PIN, money, or lunch.	Flush. Turn off water when you're finished. Return to class promptly.	Return equipment. Keep school grounds free of litter.	Arrive at school on time.	Leave promptly when dismissed. Know who is picking you up. Watch for your ride.	Be attentive.	Remember to take all belongings. Watch for your stop. Listen for bus to be called. Arrive on time. Go directly home.

SOURCE Developed in collaboration with the University of Missouri Center for School-wide Positive Behavior Support.

When using an explicit or direct instruction approach, teachers carefully plan for instruction by breaking down the social skill and developing examples and nonexamples of the skill (Mercer & Mercer, 2005; Rosenshine & Stevens, 1986). Teachers also closely monitor student performance and provide different levels of support based on student progress (Stormont, 2007). Thus, schools effectively implementing PW/SW-PBS are ensuring that all students are receiving systematic instruction on the targeted desired social behaviors versus simply assuming students will know what to do and punishing them if they engage in problem behavior. A direct or explicit instruction approach follows a predictable pattern of steps (Stormont, 2007; Meese, 2001; Rosenshine & Stevens, 1986), including the following:

- A review of the previous skill learned.
- An overview of the new social skill.
- A discussion of when, why, and where the skill is used.
- Explicit instruction on the specific behaviors that represent the skill.
- Modeling of the skill by the teacher.
- Modeling of the skill by the students.
- Practicing the skill with teacher support.
- Teacher feedback on accuracy of responding.
- Practicing the skill independently.
- Teacher feedback on accuracy of responding.
- Homework on the skill.
- Plans for generalization of skill.

Again, each specific replacement behavior listed on the matrix needs to be taught explicitly and, accordingly, lesson plans should be developed for each behavior. Figures 4.5 and 4.6 are examples of lesson plans used by teachers to teach classroom and nonclassroom behavioral expectations. Once children receive instruction on specific skills, it is also important to emphasize when such skills should or do occur in context. Highlighting the occurrence of social skills in context promotes generalization of skills. For young children, it is also important to use visual representations of the expectations. For example, a picture of a child putting toys away could represent "Be responsible," and a picture of a child giving a toy to another child could be an example of "Be kind" (Stormont, Lewis, & Beckner, 2005).

Figure 4.5 Sample lesson plan for preschool programs

Social Skills Lesson Plan

Classroom

Skill: Be safe—Use inside voice

Steps:

1. Introduce the concept that a way to be safe is to use an inside voice.

2. Teacher describes and imitates the differences between an outside and an inside voice.

3. Discuss why it is **safe**, kind, and important for the teacher and our friends to be able to hear.

4. Discuss the need or importance for quiet time, the need to use our voice so that directions can be heard, and so on.

5. Teacher should review with children through questions.

6. An attention signal, such as a raised hand, music on or off, or the light on or off, is used to cue the children when it is time to stop and listen.

Modeling/role-play

1. Teacher models inside voice.

2. Students model inside voice.

3. Teacher uses precorrects all day every day this week.

Possible materials

1. Puppets (used to demonstrate outside voice and inside voice).

   First scenario: One puppet is hurt and is calling to the teacher. The class is too loud for the teacher to hear it.

   Second scenario: Two boys are talking loudly and the group cannot hear the teacher's directions for an art activity.

Homework: Send a note home to parents telling them to ask their children to describe what an inside voice is and when to use it.

Other information:

SOURCE Developed in collaboration with the University of Missouri Center for School-wide Positive Behavior Support.

Figure 4.6   Sample lesson plan for elementary programs

SOCIAL SKILLS LESSON

Skills and Critical Rule:

- "Today we are going to talk about ways to **BE SAFE** in the classroom."

- "What are some ways we can **BE SAFE** in the classroom?"

- Ask students to define what **BEING SAFE** means. Guide their responses into observable behaviors (e.g., keep feet on ground).

- There are several ways to **BE SAFE** in the classroom. For example:
  - ○ Keep feet on ground.
  - ○ Use inside voices.
  - ○ Walk.
  - ○ Use materials safely.

  Review key behaviors and any other skills the students identify.

Demonstration and Role-Play:

Demonstrations:

- "I am going to show you some ways to **BE SAFE** and some ways to **BE UNSAFE**. I want you to watch me and see if you can tell if I am **BEING SAFE**."

- After each example, ask the students if you were **BEING SAFE**. Ask what you might do instead during nonexamples.

Examples:

- Run to seat.

- Carry scissors and pencils appropriately.

- Lean back in chair with chair feet off the floor.

- Emergency drill is pulled; move quickly to door without noise/hysteria.

_____

_____

_____

_____

(Continued)

Figure 4.6 (Continued)

Role-Plays:

- Set up a few practice sessions with your students (based on key behaviors of rule) or use older students to role-play **APPROPRIATE** examples of the skill.

- Following each role-play, review with all students.

- "Was he or she **BEING SAFE?**"

- "How do you know?"

Review and Test:

- "Today we talked about **BEING SAFE** in the classroom."

- "As you can see, there are lots of ways to **BE SAFE** in the classroom."

- Ask students to identify key behaviors for **BEING SAFE**.

Homework:

- "Today we will be watching you to see if you are **BEING SAFE** in the classroom. At the end of the day, I will ask you to tell me what you did to **BE SAFE**."

- "What should you do today?"

- "What am I going to ask you?"

SOURCE Developed in collaboration with the University of Missouri Center for School-wide Positive Behavior Support.

SUMMARY

When PW- or SW-PBS is implemented, all children have the opportunity to receive explicit instruction in appropriate social behavior. Behavior that is expected of all children is systematically determined by teams and taught. Thus, rather than focusing on developing more punitive consequences for inappropriate behavior, school staff focus on determining what appropriate behavior "looks like" in different settings, based on current problems, and initiating lesson plans to teach and support such behavior. After children are taught specific social skills, all staff need to support these behaviors, which is the focus of the next chapter.

5 Support Appropriate Behavior

Once behavior is explicitly taught to all children, educators should direct their attention to supporting desired behavior. This is another critical part of establishing a system of universal supports for all children. This support includes both prompting desired behavior and providing clear positive feedback when the behavior occurs. Overall, the environment must increase the likelihood that children will use replacement behaviors once they have been taught. If teachers teach children each behavior listed on the program's or school's matrix but the environment does not support the use of the behavior in context, then we cannot expect children to consistently demonstrate the expected behavior. For example, if children receive a well-articulated lesson (in their classroom) on using kind words in the cafeteria (e.g., "please" and "thank you") but the lunch attendants are not kind to the children, then children will probably not use these rules or behaviors in context. If children are taught to raise their hand and wait to be called on in all classes but the music teacher calls on children who do not raise their hands, children are not as likely to use and or maintain this behavior.

As discussed in previous chapters, the emphasis on teaching and supporting desired behavior is very different from traditional approaches to discipline. Appropriate behavior is not expected to emerge naturally in all students or, when it does occur, support itself (Horner & Sugai, 2005). It is also important to emphasize that each of the key features presented in this book should be viewed as interrelated and working together to support appropriate behavior and prevent problem behavior. Each feature alone would not be sufficient to support appropriate behavior in children.

Building on the instructional focus in Chapter 4, this chapter presents information on how professionals can support appropriate behavior by changing what happens in the environment before (e.g., visual prompts and cues) and after (e.g., specific behavior praise, tokens) desired behavior occurs. Several strategies are discussed and examples from preschool and elementary programs are provided. It is important to note that when children are first learning specific social behaviors, the support in the environment should be intense and frequent (Alberto & Troutman, 2003). Once children consistently demonstrate that they have learned particular social behaviors, the intensity and frequency of feedback can be adjusted accordingly.

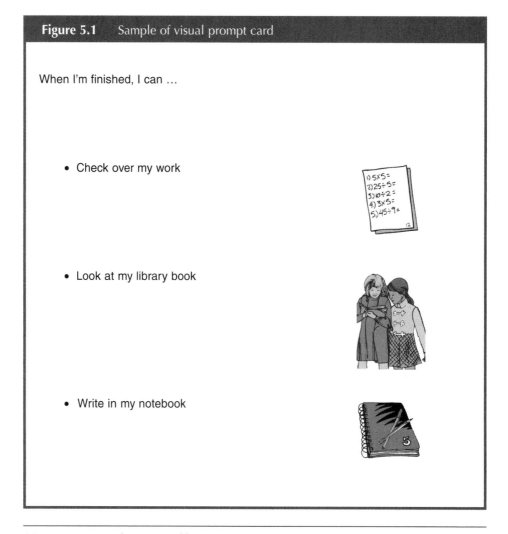

Figure 5.1   Sample of visual prompt card

When I'm finished, I can …

• Check over my work

• Look at my library book

• Write in my notebook

SOURCE Courtesy of Deanna Bickle

STRATEGIES TO INCREASE USE OF
TAUGHT BEHAVIORAL EXPECTATIONS

Prompts/Cues. Teachers can highlight appropriate behavior by providing verbal or visual prompts and cues. A visual cue could be an attention signal to indicate that children need to be quiet and listen. A visual cue could also be used to indicate the activity children should be engaged in or the activity that will be coming up next. One first-grade teacher in an elementary school implementing schoolwide positive behavioral support (SW-PBS) developed a small visual prompt card with pictures to highlight what children can do when they have completed their work (Figure 5.1). She laminated the cards and taped them to all of her children's desks.

Another school created a visual and auditory prompt to support appropriate behavior during lunchtime. Children at this particular school were talking instead of eating at lunch and then throwing away large

Figure 5.2   Reminder poster

SOURCE Courtesy of the University of Missouri Center for School-wide PBS

Figure 5.3 Visual prompt of behavioral expectations for students in the lunchroom

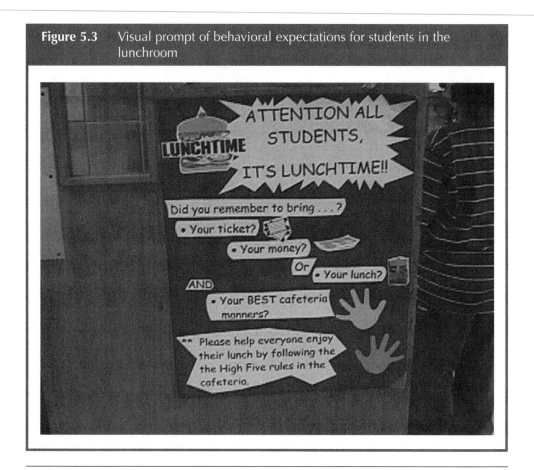

SOURCE Courtesy of the University of Missouri Center for School-wide PBS

portions of their food or asking to stay in the cafeteria to finish. As a result, music was used as an auditory cue for students. Children were taught that when the music is turned on it is time to be quiet (and finish eating lunch). A poster was also used to remind students of this routine (Figure 5.2). Students also had a visual prompt to remind them of other behavioral expectations for lunch (Figure 5.3). Visual prompts can be used to remind staff of specific routines. The same elementary school also used a visual prompt for staff to support their role in helping children transition smoothly to lunch (Figure 5.4). Visual prompts of desired behavior may include pictures of children engaging in appropriate behavior.

Proximity. Proximity is a strategy that includes the use of physical closeness to encourage appropriate behavior (Alberto & Troutman, 2003; Lampi, Fenty, & Beaunae, 2005). Teachers use proximity in the classroom

Figure 5.4 Visual prompt for teachers in the lunchroom

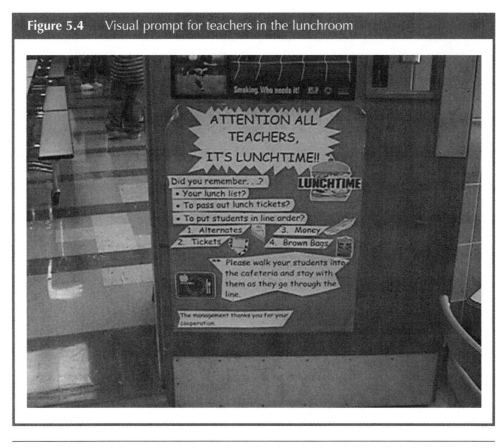

SOURCE Courtesy of the University of Missouri Center for School-wide PBS

by moving around the room frequently to check on children's engagement with activities. When teachers stand or walk next to specific children, this often increases the likelihood that children will be reminded of and redirected to appropriate behavior. For example, if Jackson is off task, the teacher could walk by his desk and pause. The physical presence of an adult may provide a nonverbal prompt for him to begin working again.

Proximity is also important to use in settings where there are a lot of children and not very many adults (Lewis et al., 2000). In these instances, it is critical that the adults who are present are actively supervising and walking around the setting, prompting skill use and providing feedback on children's appropriate behavior. Examples of settings that need active supervision include recess, cafeteria, hallways, and assemblies.

Modify Setting Factors. In many cases, certain setting factors may need to be changed to promote appropriate behavior. Teachers need to be cognizant of such environmental factors, including

- Seating arrangements (children too close together or two children who "feed off each other" seated together)
- Materials are too close to desks, and children play with them (e.g., pencil sharpener, books, markers)
- Too many children are in the block area and there are not enough blocks
- Children bringing things from home and taking them out of their cubbies or lockers at inappropriate times
- Inadequate supervision in the hallway for first recess
- Only one lunch supervisor present for first five minutes of lunch
- Last lunch period is supervised by a new teacher, who does not know the school's universal behavior expectations
- Playground monitors consistently line first-grade children up to go in from recess five minutes too early

The first four examples are classroom examples involving environmental factors that teachers can directly change (e.g., moving children, moving materials, limiting the number of children in centers, and designating specific places or rules for children's possessions). The remaining examples involve nonclassroom settings, which affect more children and teachers. The data collected by schools using PW/SW-PBS will often alert the team to potential problems. Data from the previous examples may reveal a common thread of large and disproportionate numbers of children having behavior problems given a specific setting characteristic (e.g., inadequate supervision, specific staff member who needs more professional development). As is discussed in Chapters 6 and 7, PW/SW-PBS teams collect data on children's behavior across settings and then provide more support in certain settings, with specific staff members, or with specific children.

STRATEGIES TO BUILD FLUENCY AND MAINTAIN APPROPRIATE BEHAVIOR

Verbal Feedback. After children have demonstrated appropriate behavior, they need to receive clear feedback that connects their use of specific behaviors to the universal behavioral expectations. This is part of the learning process. When children are taught a particular academic skill, teachers make sure to evaluate whether they have learned the skill and provide this feedback to children. It is also important that children receive concrete feedback regarding their social behavior. At a minimum, staff should use the school rule (replacement behavior) and the specific behavioral expectation as listed in the program's or school's matrix. Several examples of such feedback for young children include the following:

- It was *responsible* of you to bring that note back.
- It was *responsible* of you to clean up your area.
- I saw how nicely you cleaned up after yourself. That was a *responsible* thing to do.
- I noticed that you gave your glue to Rio, even though you weren't finished yet. That was *kind* of you.
- You listened when I asked for attention, which was *respectful*.
- You were being *safe* when you walked with the scissors.
- You were being *safe* when you slid down the slide on your bottom.

All staff in schools using PW/SW-PBS need to use similar language to support behavioral expectations across settings. It is also important that staff are supported in planning how to provide this feedback in an authentic way. It will not be supportive of appropriate behavior if children think people are giving them feedback in a robotic or insincere fashion.

Programwide/Schoolwide Reinforcers. Most programs and schools using systems of positive behavior support apply the principles of positive reinforcement to support increases in appropriate behavior among children. For many children, verbal feedback, which is often communicated in the form of behavior-specific praise, is both reinforcing and instructive. Often teams also choose to use additional ways to acknowledge and support positive behavior. A common strategy involves providing children with "tickets," "certificates," or a note with the verbal feedback described previously. A note may say "Caught being kind." One school used the visual prompt of a hand for "high five" to support children learning their five expectations. To support children in different settings, staff handed out paper hands when children were engaging in appropriate behavior while giving specific verbal feedback. The hands were then placed on the walls of the classroom to monitor and display their success at meeting their school's expectations.

Again, at a minimum, all staff should give specific verbal feedback (i.e., rule and specific behavioral expectation) to reinforce use of replacement behaviors. Beyond this, it is up to the program or school to develop and use other forms of reinforcement such as tickets or "gotcha" coupons, which may then be connected to other reinforcing outcomes (e.g., free time, celebrations, tangibles). Our experience has been that the PW/SW-PBS tickets are just as much about changing **staff behaviors** as student behaviors.

Teachers routinely tell us that they get busy and forget to look for and then recognize appropriate behavior, and they acknowledge inappropriate behavior only through reprimands or corrective feedback. Therefore, the tickets provide a nice prompt and result in a permanent product that can also be counted and monitored to ensure that all students are being recognized for mastering social skills (see Figures 5.5 and 5.6 for early childhood and elementary examples). It is important to emphasize that if your program or school elects to use a ticket of some sort to accompany the verbal feedback, a plan should also be in place to phase out the use of the tickets once students have built fluency in using, and staff have built fluency recognizing, replacement behaviors. When the tickets are phased out, it is important to continue to use specific verbal feedback and prompts.

Peer support strategies can also be used to encourage appropriate behavior choices in young children (Skinner, Neddenriep, Robinson, Ervin, & Jones, 2002). Classmates can support each other in many ways. Children could share observations of peers showing behavior that exemplifies the behavioral expectations at various points in the day. Teachers could provide prompts such as

- Did anyone see someone being kind at recess? What did they do?
- Did anyone see someone being a learner in art class? What was he or she doing?

Teachers could also select the behavior they want to support and narrow down the choices to something specific ("Look for and tell me about someone being kind at recess").

Researchers have recommended a more structured type of positive peer reporting referred to as *peer tootling* (Skinner et al., 2002). When using peer tootling, children are encouraged to look for positive behavior in their fellow students and then write about it. The teacher then shares this information with the class at specified times. Times for sharing may be before or after lunch, at the end of the day, or at the beginning of each day during calendar or class meeting times. Younger children could draw pictures of their classmates' appropriate behavior and then write about the event they observed in their journal. Children could share their journals and pictures with the class, the teacher, or the peer they wrote about.

Group reinforcement strategies are also used to support increases in children's use of replacement behaviors. For example, the whole class could receive a reward if children meet a particular goal. Teachers could determine what their class would be interested in earning as a reward for working

Classroom rule #1: Be Safe

I Was Caught
"Beeing"
Safe Today!

SOURCE Courtesy of the University of Missouri Center for School-wide PBS

Figure 5.6 Sample elementary certificate for demonstrating expected behavior

Certificate

I Remembered to Be Responsible!

_____
Student

_____
Teacher

_____
Date

SOURCE Courtesy of the University of Missouri Center for School-wide PBS

toward specific behavior goals as a class. To use group contingencies, teachers need to (Alberto & Troutman, 2003; Mercer & Mercer, 2005)

1. Identify one or more behavioral goals that the class as a whole, or a percentage of the class, needs to work on.

   Example: A preschool class has been explicitly taught and prompted to be kind on the playground and to line up the first time asked. However, this class continues to have trouble coming in from outside when prompted, and teachers have to prompt children, on average, five times.

   Example: A third-grade class has been explicitly taught by their classroom teacher to be respectful in art class and to listen to the teacher when she asks for their attention. However, this class continues to have difficulty paying attention in art class, and a large percentage of the class fails to complete their assignments appropriately.

2. Identify setting factors that may need to be changed.

3. Talk with children about the problem behavior and set goals for improvement.

4. Clearly state what you want children to do instead (the replacement behavior) and teach this behavior (see Chapter 4).

5. Determine what children would like to earn for reaching their class goal.

6. Help children set high but reasonable goals (e.g., the number of tickets according to current data).

7. Remind children daily of class goal and class reward.

8. Monitor progress toward goal daily and share data on progress with class.

Young children may want to earn simple rewards on a daily basis for meeting their class goal. Perhaps the preschool class in the former example decides, with teacher assistance, that if they come in from outside the first time asked both times they go outside, then they all get to have a special treat from the treat box when they leave for the day. Her treat box includes small, inexpensive items that the preschoolers like. The preschool teacher uses prompts and specific praise when children come in the first time asked and plans to phase out the treat box reward after children build fluency coming in the first time asked. For young children, the use of hand stamps when a class goal is met is another inexpensive and simple way to reinforce behavior. They could also be encouraged to share with their families the reason they received hand stamps. Another example of a group contingency that one early childhood program uses includes placing teacher-made bees in a teacher-made bee hive and announcing the appropriate behavior that was observed, leading to the awarding of a bee. Then, when a certain number of bees are in the bee hive, the class stops and sings a song and has a little celebration.

In the second example, the third-grade class struggling in art class decides that they would like 15 minutes of free time to play class games on Friday if they complete their work in art class each week. On the basis of the current performance of the class, which reflects that only 50% of the class is completing the assignments, the teacher and students decide that at least 90% of students need to complete their work to earn the reward. The teacher works with the art teacher to decide how they can monitor this together. They decide that students will receive tickets from the art teacher when they complete their in-class or homework assignments for the week. To meet the class goal of 90% completion, 20 of the 25 students have to turn in tickets to their teacher by Friday morning.

Review Often. It is imperative that staff understand that learning and maintaining social behavior is very similar to maintaining academic skills. Most teachers acknowledge the importance of reviewing prerequisite content before beginning a new unit that builds on this content. Social skills also need to be reviewed often and connected to new social skills. In addition, it is important to note that reviews of expected social behavior should be intensified after breaks and long weekends. Such reviews proactively support children's use of appropriate behavior. Chapter 6 further discusses the importance of using review and reteaching as a consequence for "social errors."

SUMMARY

Children need a lot of prompts and feedback, especially when they are first learning new social behaviors. This chapter included strategies that professionals can use to set children up for success by promoting the use of appropriate behavior. Support strategies addressed in this chapter include providing prompts, cues, environmental changes, and clear feedback and reinforcement structures for increasing the likelihood that children will use and maintain appropriate social behaviors. Just like the process for academic learning, children need to understand which skills are important to use in specific contexts, and they need the opportunity to practice and receive feedback.

6 Corrective Consequences

W hen students are explicitly taught what it looks like to be kind, safe, responsible, or respectful, and then receive prompts and reinforcement for using appropriate behavior, they are less likely to engage in problem behavior (Lewis & Sugai, 1999; Sugai et al., 2000). Chapters 4 and 5 addressed how schools and programs can teach and then support appropriate replacement behaviors. However, even when programs and schools use a positive proactive approach to teaching and supporting appropriate behavior, problem behavior will still occur. When problem behavior occurs, it is important to know how to address it and to have clear consequences in place, as well as steps to prevent the problem behavior from occurring in the future. Teams need to drive this process and ensure that three factors are considered. First, problem behavior needs to be clearly defined and corrected consistently. Second, problem behavior needs to be consistently documented to drive decision making. Third, problem behavior needs to guide the implementation of corrective consequences.

DEFINING AND CONSISTENTLY RESPONDING TO PROBLEM BEHAVIOR

Consistent responding to problem behavior is a very important universal support strategy and a key feature of programwide/schoolwide positive behavior support (PW/SW-PBS). Many schools have a set of consequences they often use, which may be included in their discipline policy. However, the terminology used in discipline policies may be very different from the proactive, positive, and instructional language used when implementing PW/SW-PBS, and the behaviors described in the policy may be subjective and open to different interpretations. The team should review these policies to determine their fit with PBS efforts. The goal of evaluating current practices is to create a universal system in which all staff members respond to problem behavior in a *consistent* and *instructional* manner.

As such, the team should first define problem behaviors, such as classroom disruption and disrespect toward adults, in measurable and observable terms. When defining problem behaviors, the team should determine the common definitions used by staff and come to consensus on specific definitions. The team will need to discuss each type of behavior and then present its definitions to the teaching staff for further clarification. The key is to determine common definitions of misbehavior and describe this behavior in relation to PBS expectations. Thus, although staff agree on problem behavior and corresponding consequences, they are also discussing the replacement behaviors for instruction.

It is also important for teams to support consistency in how adults respond to problem behavior. Consistent rules and consequences for *all students* across *all settings* and with *all staff members* help children learn which behaviors are expected and will be acknowledged and which are not acceptable. Staff must enforce the rules. When some staff members allow talking in line at the bathroom but others do not, children may be confused and/or have difficulty demonstrating appropriate bathroom behavior consistently. Teams must also establish procedures to be used consistently by all staff, including, for example, what behaviors warrant within-classroom management and what behaviors should be managed in a behavior/detention room or the office (or, in preschool programs, perhaps a safe spot). One early childhood program team developed a behavior flow chart to prompt staff to use specific procedures when responding to children's problem behavior (Figure 6.1). The basic logic of the flow chart is to prompt staff to exhaust proactive strategies before corrective steps and to match the intensity of the response to the intensity of the behavior.

DOCUMENTATION OF PROBLEM BEHAVIOR

Data-based decision making is a critical feature of PW/SW-PBS that is expanded on in Chapter 7. To support decision making regarding problem behavior and teaching needs, data collection forms are used. Examples of an elementary office discipline referral (ODR) form and an early childhood behavior incident report are shown in Figures 6.2 and 6.3. It is important to note that most elementary schools already have office disciplinary referral forms in place for children who engage in problem behavior that results

Figure 6.1 Behavior flow chart

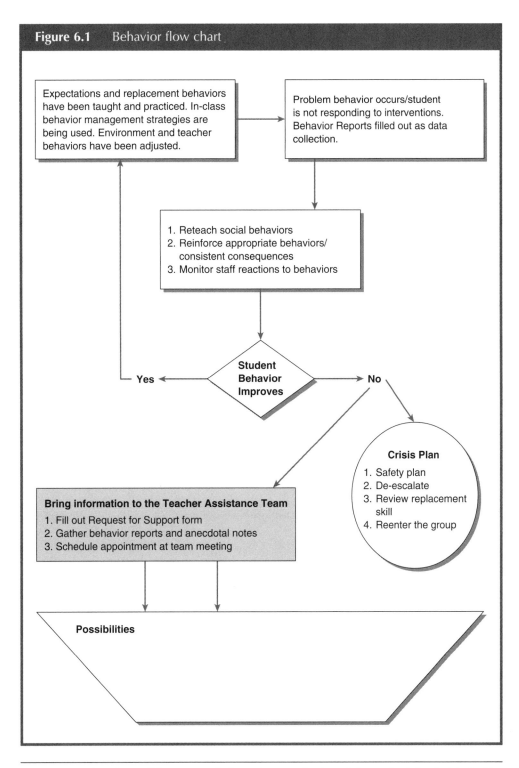

Expectations and replacement behaviors have been taught and practiced. In-class behavior management strategies are being used. Environment and teacher behaviors have been adjusted.

Problem behavior occurs/student is not responding to interventions. Behavior Reports filled out as data collection.

1. Reteach social behaviors
2. Reinforce appropriate behaviors/ consistent consequences
3. Monitor staff reactions to behaviors

Student Behavior Improves

Yes

No

Crisis Plan
1. Safety plan
2. De-escalate
3. Review replacement skill
4. Reenter the group

Bring information to the Teacher Assistance Team
1. Fill out Request for Support form
2. Gather behavior reports and anecdotal notes
3. Schedule appointment at team meeting

Possibilities

SOURCE Developed in collaboration with the University of Missouri Center for School-wide Positive Behavior Support.

Figure 6.2 Example of an elementary school office referral form

EXAMPLE OF AN ELEMENTARY BEHAVIOR REPORT

Student: _____ □ Student receives SPED services   Student's teacher: _____

Grade: PK K 1 2 3 4 5   Date: _____   Time: _____   Reporting Staff: _____

Location: □ Bathroom □ Bus zone/parent pickup □ Cafeteria □ Classroom □ Gym
□ Hallway □ Media center □ On bus □ Playground □ Special event/assembly/field trip

Others involved: □ None □ Peers □ Staff □ Teacher □ Substitute □ Other

Motivation: □ Obtain peer attention □ Obtain adult attention □ Obtain items/activity
□ Avoid peers □ Avoid adults □ Avoid task or activity □ Revenge/power struggle

Antecedent activity: □ Leisure/solitary □ Leisure/social □ Transition □ Academic solo work
□ Academic group work

Trigger: □ Asked to perform a task □ Given repeated directions □ Conflict with peers
□ Teacher working with others □ Specific academic activity □ Provoked by peers
□ Presence of specific peers □ Ignored by peers □ _____

Teacher interventions: Check all that apply
□ Prompt/redirection given □ Reteaching of rule/routine □ Behavior choices given
□ Safe spot in room □ Get control pass □ Privileges removed □ Think sheet
□ Conference with student □ Buddy room
□ Parents contacted via: □ Phone □ Mail □ Folder □ e-mail □ Left message
   Person contacted: _____

MINOR behavior:	MAJOR behavior:	Administrative action:
□ Defiance/disrespect/ noncompliance 1 2 3	□ Abusive language	□ Conference with parents
□ Disruption 1 2 3	□ Alcohol/drugs/tobacco/weapon	□ Conference with student
□ Tease/bullying	□ Arson	□ Expulsion
□ Inapprop. language	□ Defiance/disrespect/noncompliance	□ Individualized instruction
□ Physical contact	□ Disruption	□ In-school suspension
□ Property misuse or damage	□ Fighting/physical aggression	□ Loss of privileges
	□ Harassment/teasing/taunting/bullying	□ Out-of-school suspension
	□ Lying	□ PBS team referral
	□ Property damage	**Other comments:**
	□ Theft	_____
		_____

□ **Copy to teacher**	Brief description of incident: _____
□ **Copy to school resource officer**	_____
□ **Entered into schoolwide information system**	_____

Parents: If this form is a Major Behavior Report, it is being sent home for you to keep. It reports what we spoke about on the phone. If we were unable to reach you by phone, we have sent two copies. Please sign one copy and return it to school tomorrow so that we know you received it. You may keep the other copy.

_____ _____   _____ _____
Teacher's signature   Date   Student's signature   Date

_____ _____   _____ _____
Administrator's signature Date   Parent's signature   Date

NOTES SPED = special education; PBS = positive behavior support

SOURCE Developed in collaboration with the University of Missouri Center for School-wide Positive Behavior Support.

Figure 6.3   Example of an early childhood behavior incident report

Incident # ____   **Early Childhood Behavior Incident Report**   **IEP yes/no**

Child's name _____ Classroom teacher _____

Person reporting _____ Date _____ Time _____

Descriptive information should go on another sheet. A separate incident = the child is engaged in an activity with appropriate behavior for 15+ minutes before behavior is repeated or another problem behavior is demonstrated.

Number the initial behavior, response, and outcome. Make note of event order after the initial behavior.

Problem behavior	Location	Others involved
Externalizing ____ Physical aggression ____ Inappropriate language ____ Property destruction **Internalizing** ____ Crying, whining throughout an activity ____ Isolated play after prompt to join others **Noncompliance** ____ Refusals ____ Disruption of learning **Self-abuse/ stimulation** **Other:** _____	____ Structured classroom activity ____ Unstructured classroom activity ____ Transition ____ Hallway ____ Playground ____ Bus ____ Other: _____	____ Peer(s) ____ Teacher ____ Aide ____ Specialist ____ Bus driver ____ Substitute ____ Administration ____ Others: _____ _____

Initial trigger for behavior	Response to behavior
____ Adult request/redirection ____ Unstructured play ____ Peer provoked ____ Difficult task ____ Adult not in close proximity ____ No peer attention ____ Other: _____	**Attention** ____ Adult verbal attention ____ Adult physical attention ____ Adult eye contact ____ Peer verbal attention ____ Peer physical attention **Ignore** ____ Adult ignored behavior ____ Peer ignored behavior ____ Sensory strategy: ____ Other: _____
Comments:	**Comments:**

NOTE IEP = individualized education plan

SOURCE Developed in collaboration with the University of Missouri Center for School-wide Positive Behavior Support.

in being sent to the office. However, schools may not have clear consensus regarding which behaviors warrant an ODR, how ODRs should be used to inform instructional needs, or other ways ODR data are used. Thus, it is important that the team supports the use of these best practices. It is also important to note that most early childhood programs do not, and typically should not, use ODRs. However, the development of some type of form allows the PBS team to track information about specific settings, individual students, and teachers who may need more support.

Definitions of behaviors that are decided on by the team could be listed on the back of the data collection forms for staff to reference. In addition to the type of problem behavior, data collection forms typically include the following information:

- Location of the incident
- Time of the incident
- Individuals involved
- Possible antecedents (trigger or prompt) for the behavior
- Consequences for the behavior
- Suspected motivation for the behavior (e.g., getting or avoiding something)

All of these pieces of data can provide information for selecting interventions. For example, if a second-grade student tears down a poster (behavior) in the classroom (location) after the teacher (who was involved) gives the group an assignment (antecedent activity), and the student is then sent to the "buddy room" (teacher intervention), the team can hypothesize that the problem behavior may have occurred because the student was attempting to avoid the task (motivation).

USING CORRECTIVE CONSEQUENCES

The process of responding to problem behavior is much like an error analysis, which is commonly used for academic work. When using error analysis, teachers are examining student work carefully to determine what types of problems students are having and then using this information to inform instruction. For example, if a student follows the steps needed to solve a problem in math but makes computational errors, then he or she does not need to be retaught the steps but rather needs to practice basic math facts. If teachers do not perform error analyses, they do not know where children's skill deficits are and will likely reteach children things they already know.

Social error analyses will also inform staff of the specific type of social skills deficits, which will again inform instruction. Children can have social skills deficits or performance problems (Sugai & Lewis, 1996). When children have a **skill deficit**, they have not learned a skill to fluency or have not maintained the skill. Accordingly, children will need more explicit instruction and practice. When children have a **performance problem**, they have learned a particular social skill but are not using it consistently or in all appropriate settings. In these instances, children need more prompts and cues to highlight the need for the replacement behavior in context and may need more intense reinforcement when they use the replacement behavior. In addition to exploring instructional needs of children, the environment also needs to be closely examined for potential changes.

Overall, problem behavior is carefully examined to determine instructional and environmental needs. If children have skill deficits or performance problems, this information is used to embed instruction more carefully and to create more support for children to use replacement behaviors. Accordingly, specific types of corrective consequences will include

- Reteaching children replacement behavior and providing more practice.
- Providing additional support (e.g., increasing cues and providing stronger reinforcement) for the desired behavior in specific settings.
- Targeting classroom or other setting conditions that may be supporting the use of the problem behavior (e.g., staff members are not prompting desired replacement behaviors, staff members are not using positive feedback when children use replacement behaviors).

Data collected from the behavioral reports describing who is engaging in problem behavior, the type of behavior, settings, and so forth should help inform which corrective consequence(s) is needed. For example, if a small group of children is demonstrating a specific problem behavior, such as jumping down the stairwell, the teacher should reteach with the small group of children. In this case, appropriate instruction would include

- Reteaching the behavioral expectation (how to walk safely down the stairs).
- Practicing the expected skill in the hallway.
- Providing verbal acknowledgment and additional and perhaps more intense reinforcers for demonstration of replacement behavior.

If only one student demonstrated a problem behavior, the appropriate action would still be to reteach the expectation, practice the appropriate behavior, and acknowledge demonstration of the correct response with verbal feedback. The only difference is that the teacher would reteach the behavior with only the child who is having problems. Finally, if problem behavior occurs frequently when children are with one person or in one setting (playground), then the adults need to be questioned and the setting examined for potential modifications and support needs. Using data to drive professional development needs was a focus of Chapter 3 and is revisited in greater detail in Chapter 7.

Another corrective and research-based strategy that incorporates the behavioral supports presented in this chapter and in Chapters 4 and 5, including using prompts, proximity, analysis of setting factors, positive reinforcement, and social skills instruction, is **precorrection** (Lampi et al., 2005; Walker et al., 2004). When teachers use this instructional strategy, they are setting the occasion for appropriate behavior by providing reminders and modifying any environmental factors that support problem behavior. Even though precorrection is often used in response to problem behavior, it is best used proactively when working with problem behavior. Reminding children of the behavior expectations before they transition to a new setting or task that in the past has been problematic is a powerful behavioral management strategy. Specific steps for using precorrection and an example follow (Lampi et al., 2005; Walker et al., 2004).

- **Step 1:** Target the setting where problem behavior tends to occur.
- **Step 2**: Determine what you want the children to do instead of the current behavior.
- **Step 3:** Determine and then change any environmental factors that seem to support the problem behavior.
- **Step 4**: Teach the appropriate behavior explicitly.
- **Step 5**: Support the appropriate behavior through positive reinforcement.
- **Step 6**: Prompt for appropriate behavior before entering the setting or starting an activity.
- **Step 7**: Monitor children's progress.

Recess Is Over

Mrs. Jackson's first-grade class bounces in after their afternoon recess. She is planning for the next day and can hear them yelling and running down the hall. Before she can get to the door, three children have already engaged in a game of leapfrog and bounced into the classroom one over the other. As she attempts to manage their behavior, the other children come in noisily and do not go to their desks. After turning off the lights and providing 10 prompts for children to go to their desks and put their heads down, 15 minutes have passed since the children came in from recess. Mrs. Jackson consults with the SW-PBS team, and they suggest the use of precorrection. As a result, she follows the seven steps outlined previously.

1. **Target the setting where problem behavior tends to occur.** Transition from afternoon recess.

2. **Determine what you want the children to do instead of the current behavior.**
   - Walk down the hall.
   - Use peaceful voices.
   - Enter the classroom quietly.
   - Go to their desks.
   - Get out their writing journals.

3. **Determine and then change any environmental factors that seem to be supporting the problem behavior.** Mrs. Jackson feels that the lack of adult supervision in the hallway is contributing to her children's behavior in the hall, which then contributes to their behavior when they enter her classroom. As a result, she meets her students at the end of the hall and prompts them to walk down the hall and use peaceful voices.

4. **Explicitly teach the appropriate behavior.** Mrs. Jackson teaches her students the appropriate behaviors that represent the new routine of entering from recess in the afternoon. She uses an explicit instruction strategy (see Chapter 4), with concrete skills explained, modeled, and practiced. Students practice the entire routine that morning and then practice again right before afternoon recess.

5. **Support the appropriate behavior through positive reinforcement.** Mrs. Jackson's class loves to play large-group games. Mrs. Jackson tells her class that if they follow the new recess routine they will play a quick class game of their choice at the end of the day.

6. **Prompt for appropriate behavior.** Mrs. Jackson uses nonverbal and visual prompts as the students enter the building following recess. She meets her children in the hallway and has her finger over her mouth to prompt for quiet voices. She also has posted a visual prompt on her door that has a picture of a desk and journal on it.

7. **Monitor children's progress.** Mrs. Jackson takes notes regarding the success of the new routine. Of her students, 18 are consistently following the routine and two are having some problems. Mrs. Jackson provides more support for these two students, including more practice and using proximity in the hallway and when the two children enter the classroom.

Overall, when using PW/SW-PBS, staff should always have an eye toward what children should be doing instead and how to increase the likelihood that they will engage in appropriate behavior. Thus, there is a strong focus on using consequences to promote appropriate behavior. Consider traditional approaches that do not work with children at risk for antisocial behavior. Remember these are *nonexamples.*

Sorting Skittles in the Buddy Room

Philip, a third grader, was sent to the buddy room for being disruptive in class. He was there for 10 minutes, given a sheet that he didn't fill out, and dismissed to go back to his class when his time was up. When he returned to his classroom, his teacher asked him what he did in the buddy room, hoping to have a conversation about his behavior; he said, "I sorted Skittles into colors." "Who gave you Skittles?" his teacher asked. "Mrs. Foster, in the buddy room."

Philip Hates Math

Almost every day, Philip engages in yelling and waving his hands during independent seat work time in math. Almost every day, as a consequence, his teacher sends him to the buddy room. Philip converses with Mrs. Foster, who routinely gives him a small package of Skittles. Mrs. Foster has never received information on how to support Philip in the buddy room. She feels she is only a supervisor, and she tracks the time he is in there and then dismisses him.

Programs and schools have many different ways for handling different types of behavior problems and may use these sorts of exclusionary consequences. It is critical that PBS teams help staff and systems support the use of corrective consequences for problem behavior. The information from Philip's experiences should be carefully noted and given to the PBS team for decision making. In these examples, the following needs for support are noted:

- The team needs to assist Philip's teacher in determining, teaching, and supporting replacement behaviors.
- Mrs. Foster needs support for learning her role in the buddy room. The team needs to develop a plan for providing this support.

ADDITIONAL CONSIDERATIONS

Consider Development. Developmental considerations must be made when addressing consequences in early childhood settings. Just as there is a difference between expected behaviors of kindergarteners versus fifth graders, it is also important to emphasize the difference when comparing three- and four-year-olds with elementary students. Many preschool-age children have never been in settings where appropriate school behaviors have been taught and will need extensive practice and feedback on their behavior. Also, there is a wider range of what is considered to be typical behavior for young children. It is developmentally appropriate for three-year-olds to throw tantrums when they are tired or upset. The goals of PW-PBS are the same as those for SW-PBS: children need to be taught appropriate behavior (e.g., better ways to deal with frustrating events). However, young children's communication skills will affect their ability to express what they desire or what they find frustrating. The teacher should support young children by helping them choose words to express themselves. For children with less developed language, teachers can provide an **alternative communication method**, such as a picture schedule.

Determining Different Consequences for Unique Needs. Data collected on problem behavior and consequences provide the team with (a) information on staff members who need further training or assistance in implementing strategies and (b) the identification of and needed supports for students with chronic concerns. An early childhood behavioral consultant developed the behavioral checklist presented in Figure 6.4 so she could target children who may need more support.

Other responsibilities of the PBS team include the development of program policies (e.g., regarding the number of times a student can be sent to the buddy room before the teacher is asked to consult the teacher assistance team or the student is referred for more intense supports). This topic is discussed in greater detail in Chapter 8.

Figure 6.4 Early childhood behavior checklist

Early Childhood Behavior Checklist

Child's name _____ Teacher's name _____

Date of screening _____ Child's age _____ IEP* __ Yes __ No

Please rate each of the following based on the child's current developmental level:

The child generally...	Age-appropriate	Possible concern	Definite concern
1. Complies with rules and directions.			
2. Follows daily preschool routines.			
3. Participates in clean-up when asked to do so.			
4. Attends to group activities.			
5. Interacts socially with others.			
6. Keeps hands and feet to self.			
7. Has friends.			
8. Demonstrates an appropriate range of emotions.			
9. Handles frustration appropriately.			
10. Appears happy and content to be at school.			
11. Controls temper in conflict situations or when doesn't get his or her own way.			
12. Demonstrates appropriate activity level for age.			
13. Separates well from family.			
14. Adapts to changes in environment/schedule.			
15. Requests assistance/comfort when needed.			

*Child receives special education or related services.

Comments (to include environmental/family concerns):

NOTE IEP = individualized education plan

SOURCE Developed in collaboration with the University of Missouri Center for School-wide Positive Behavior Support.

SUMMARY

This chapter addresses the importance of consistent and proactive consequences for problem behavior. The establishment of clear communication regarding behaviors and corresponding consequences is essential for the success of PW/SW-PBS. Consequences are administered with a focus on teaching more appropriate behavior. Because problem behavior can be considered a learning error, the natural response should be to review and practice the rules and to provide feedback on behavioral corrections. Policies and procedures developed by the PBS team will drive decision making regarding consequences and supports for staff and students alike. Chapter 7 will further address the role of the team in the collection of useful data and analysis for decision making.

7 Data-Based Decision Making

To ensure the systematic implementation of the key features discussed throughout this book, including defining expectations, teaching expected behaviors directly to students, and providing support and corrective consequences, a continuous process of data collection and analysis must be implemented. Within effective systems of programwide/schoolwide positive behavior support (PW/SW-PBS), student behavior is continuously monitored, and the data are used by staff to make decisions, sometimes with the guidance of a PW/SW coach (Scott & Martinek, 2006; Sugai & Horner, 1996). The collection and analysis of data for decision making are primary, ongoing responsibilities of the PBS team.

By using a systematic process of data collection and analysis, teams can determine where their focus should be for systems change efforts while simultaneously increasing the likelihood that these efforts will be efficient and effective (Lewis-Palmer, Sugai, & Larson, 1999). For both early childhood programs and elementary schools, PBS teams must be strategic in developing a systematic process for data-based decision making that begins with identifying the problems they face, which in turn leads to intervention plan development. Teams also use data to ascertain the integrity of implementation of the interventions (e.g., are teachers actually using the recommended strategies in an appropriate manner?). Data collection eventually culminates with the evaluation of the strengths and remaining challenges of the interventions that have been implemented. This systematic decision-making process can be used at all levels: schoolwide universal systems, secondary support systems, and individual systems. Secondary support systems and individual systems are described in detail in Chapter 8.

DESIGNING A PLAN FOR DATA COLLECTION

The role of the PW/SW-PBS team in data collection and analysis is multi-faceted. The team must develop a plan that begins by addressing the following questions:

1. What questions would the PW/SW-PBS team like answered?

2. What information will help the PW/SW-PBS team answer these questions?

3. What information does the building or PW/SW-PBS team already typically collect?

4. What new information does the PW/SW-PBS team need?

Next, the PW/SW-PBS team must decide who will be responsible for data collection, when they will collect the data and in what format, and who will be responsible for entry of data into a database. Finally, the team must implement a consistent data analysis process that leads to decision making and intervention planning to address the questions originally posed by the team.

Defining Questions. The first task for the PW/SW-PBS team is to identify the questions they have. These questions will guide the process of data collection and analysis. Typical team questions fall into the basic categories of (a) defining problems (e.g., by examining data, teams might decide they have a problem with aggression on the playground, but they need to know the time of day, number of students involved, whether the students are repeated users of aggression, and whether these students are new to the school or returning students); (b) developing integrity of implementation plans and determining the impact of plan implementation; and (c) in some cases individual (i.e., student or teacher) problem solving.

Identifying Standard Data Sources. The second step is to identify the information or data the building or program collects as a matter of standard practice over the course of the day, week, month, or year. It is important for the team to determine whether they can answer any of the identified questions using this data. If they can, the team needs to identify when these data are collected and who is responsible for collecting and collating these data. This informs the team about whether or not the data will be available when they want or need to initiate the decision-making process and with whom to collaborate in order to access the data.

Identifying Other Data Sources. The third step is to identify data the team needs beyond the already available data set to address their questions. Teams should consider four general types of data in their decision making: (a) archival, (b) rating/survey, (c) interview, and (d) observational. **Archival data** include items that are produced by students or written or collected by others. This is the most common form of data available to SW/PBS teams because it encompasses the typical data that schools collect. Archival data in K–3 programs might include student and teacher demographic information, student attendance, student achievement (both standardized measures and teacher-developed assessments), and disciplinary referrals (e.g., "safe seat," buddy room, or office referrals) that result in measurement of student time out of instruction. Archival data in Pre–K programs include the same sources available in elementary schools with the exception of office/disciplinary referrals. However, preschool programs could use another source of archival data (e.g., behavioral incident forms) to track problem behavior in their programs.

The three final types of data are not typically collected by all schools but are data sources that can be easily collected. **Rating scales** and **surveys** provide perceptual data that allow teams to assess staff, student, and parental opinions regarding PW/SW-PBS efforts. When intervention efforts are perceived positively, they have a level of social validity. Examples of parent, teacher, and student PBS social validity surveys are presented in Figures 7.1, 7.2, and 7.3.

Interviews are similar to ratings scales and surveys, but they also allow for further probing and exploration based on the interviewee's answers. See Figure 7.4 for a further illustration of the variety of data sources from each of the four categories of data sources for early childhood and elementary PBS implementation.

Data Collection Responsibilities. The fourth step in implementing a systematic decision-making process is to identify the individual responsible for collecting and entering data into a database. Deciding who collects the data will depend in part on job roles, flexibility of time, and access to data sources. Development, copying, and distribution of surveys can be done by almost anyone. Data entry is dependent on time, access to, and knowledge of different types of databases and appropriate data analyses. Utilization of computer-based data programs is highly recommended.

Data Collection Schedule. The fifth step is to devise a schedule that ensures that designated data are collected. PW/SW-PBS teams need to plan strategically by working backward. Accordingly, teams need to pinpoint the last date possible for data to be turned in for respective decision

(Text continues on page 102)

Figure 7.1   Parent positive behavior support social validity survey

POSITIVE BEHAVIOR SUPPORT PARENT SURVEY

Answer each question below by marking a response:

1 = Yes   2 = Sometimes/neutral   3 = No

	1	2	3
1. My child talks about the school rules and expectations.			
2. Most of the students at my child's school follow the school rules and expectations.			
3. The school provides me with information about the school rules and expectations.			
4. My child is taught the school rules and expectations.			
5. My child feels safe in all areas of the school (hallways, bathrooms, commons, playground).			
6. My child's teacher(s) recognizes my child for following the school rules and expectations.			
7. I want the school to continue teaching schoolwide rules and expectations next year.			

Thank you for your ideas! Please return this form to your child's teacher.

SOURCE Developed in collaboration with the University of Missouri Center for School-wide Positive Behavior Support.

Figure 7.2   Teacher positive behavior support social validity survey

POSITIVE BEHAVIOR SUPPORT STAFF SOCIAL VALIDITY SURVEY

Indicate the number of years you have worked for the district:

1–5___ 6–10___ 11–20___ 21+ ___

Please circle the number that reflects your level of agreement with the following statements (1 = yes; 2 = sometimes/neutral; 3 = no):

1. My administrator(s) actively supports PBS (e.g., PBS is on staff meeting agendas, attends PBS meeting, accesses resources to promote PBS).

    1   2   3

2. The PBS team in my building has provided the necessary support to implement PBS (e.g., lesson plans, when to teach, how to teach).

    1   2   3

3. Technical support and information are provided to implement PBS (e.g., coaches' training, assistance from district PBS facilitators).

    1   2   3

4. Data are collected, analyzed, and shared with staff on a regular basis.

    1   2   3

5. Opportunities exist to provide feedback on PBS to the team and administration.

    1   2   3

6. The PBS strategies have been easily embedded into the school day (e.g., teaching, reinforcing, giving precorrects).

    1   2   3

7. My students would say that I give frequent positive feedback when they follow the rules.

    1   2   3

8. This school should continue to implement PBS.

    1   2   3

9. Student behavior, in general, has improved at our school.

    1   2   3

SOURCE Developed in collaboration with the University of Missouri Center for School-wide Positive Behavior Support.

Figure 7.3 Student positive behavior support social validity survey

POSITIVE BEHAVIOR SUPPORT ELEMENTARY STUDENT SURVEY

The Expectations: Students Are Safe, Kind, Respectful Learners!

0	0	0	0	0
1	1	1	1	1
2	2	2	2	2
3	3	3	3	3
4	4	4	4	4
5	5	5	5	5
6	6	6	6	6
7	7	7	7	7
8	8	8	8	8
9	9	9	9	9

Please pencil in the squares for your student ID number. This is the same number you use at lunch.

For the next seven items, check the box with the number of the answer you agree with: 1 = yes; 2 = sometimes; 3 = no.

	1	2	3
1. I feel safe at school.			
2. Students at my school treat each other respectfully.			
3. Having the expectations makes it easier for me to learn.			
4. My teacher teaches me about the expectations.			
5. Teachers let me know when I follow the expectations.			
6. When I am home and in the community I follow the expectations taught at school.			
7. I like school.			

Thank you for your ideas!

SOURCE Developed in collaboration with the University of Missouri Center for School-wide Positive Behavior Support.

Figure 7.4   Positive behavior support data sources

Type	Data source	Description	Programwide	Schoolwide
A	Attendance	Data collected by schools on a daily or hourly basis.	X	X
A	Demographics	Data collected by schools or programs that can include gender, ethnicity, socioeconomic status, special needs status.	X	X
A	Disciplinary referrals	Data collected by schools or programs should include date, time, referring adult, location, type of behavior, other individuals involved, and possible motivation entered into a database such as SWIS (see www.swis.org).	X	X
A	Developmental milestones	Data collected on social, emotional, cognitive, academic, and motor development.	X	X
A	Achievement	Academic achievement can be collected through teacher developed checklists or tests, standardized checklists or tests, or product assessment through the use of a rubric.	X	X
I/O	Schoolwide Evaluation Tool	Research tool to be used by trained evaluator. Observation and interviews are used to assess the spread of the PBS intervention within the context of the program in question.	NA	X
R	Effective Behavior Support Survey	Staff survey of universals, nonclassroom, small-group, and individual levels of PBS; standardized tool available online.	NA	X
R	Social Validity Survey	School or program generated to assess stakeholders' opinions of the value of the PBS (see examples from PBS).	X	X
O	Observation by team members, administrators, or staff members	School- or program-generated observation protocol to assess • Implementation of intervention • Student behavior	X	X
I	Interviews by team members, administrators, or staff members	School- or program-generated or standardized interview protocol to assess • Stakeholders' opinions • Stakeholder implementation	X	X

NOTES SWIS = Schoolwide Information System; PBS = positive behavior support; A = archival; R = rating scale/survey; I = interview; O = observation making. Additionally, planning adequate time for data to be collected (e.g., time for completion of a survey) increases the likelihood that data will be turned in before the deadline. A distribution date can be identified using the time needed for completion/collection as a guide. The distribution date provides the timeline for an instrument, such as a survey, or a process, such as interviews, to be developed so that it will be ready for distribution or implemented on the date established. Using incentives can increase response rates for both students and staff.

Data Analysis. The final step in an efficient data-based decision-making process involves data analysis. Appropriate analyses are determined by the original questions posed by the PBS team and the types of data sources. In most cases, data will be analyzed to determine frequencies or averages. For example, teams can review responses to interviews to determine different barriers to implementation efforts (e.g., teachers report they do not feel they have time to support individual children with behavior problems). Teams can also review surveys to determine the overall mood of staff and parents regarding the use of PW/SW-PBS. If the overall perception is negative, teams will want to further support professional development for teachers and outreach efforts for parents. Teacher observations can identify the frequency of use for target key behavior supports (e.g., precorrection, positive verbal feedback, use of corrective consequences).

For each type of data, PBS teams must decide what they will consider as evidence of a positive, beneficial, or meaningful change or effect. One widely accepted indicator that universal levels of intervention are *effective* is a reduction in office disciplinary referrals (ODRs) or behavioral infractions. The team should set goals from baseline to implementation and monitor progress toward their goals (Bambara & Kern, 2005). By adopting an indicator level for positive impacts, whether recommended by individual school, district, or national norms, the PBS team has a guide by which to decide whether the intervention is working. Overall, there should be multiple sources of data from the four general categories (e.g., archival, ratings scales/surveys, interviews, and observations) to use for decision making.

SW-PBS DECISION MAKING

Integrity of SW-PBS Implementation. Whether focusing at the school-wide, small-group, or individual level, PBS teams begin by first posing and answering questions related to the most pressing challenges or problems to be solved and developing interventions intended to address the challenges.

Once the PW/SW-PBS intervention plan has been developed, agreed on, and implemented, the PBS team must assess the integrity of implementation. The team would optimally have multiple sources of data to assess plan implementation, including the following school-developed measures:

- Observational data to assess how often teachers or supervisors use recommended strategies (e.g., teach lessons for the new rules or routines, prompt for expectations, give positive feedback, or provide corrective consequences).
- Survey data to determine the dates and times that teachers use key features (e.g., taught a new routine or rule).
- Interview data to clarify survey or observation data.
- Archival data to determine when certain events took place (e.g., logs of training dates for the playground supervisors, copies of the playground lesson plans distributed to staff members).
- Artifacts that document implementation of key behavior supports (e.g., lesson plans or schedules for teaching lessons, visual signs with rules or routines, and training materials for playground supervisors and teachers).

Additional assessment tools teams can use to assess plan implementation include the Effective Behavior Support Survey (available at www .pbis.org/tools.htm). This survey can be used to assess staff members' opinions regarding schoolwide, nonclassroom, classroom, secondary, and individual-level PBS implementation. A preschool version of this survey was discussed in Chapter 3 as a tool that can be used by teams for a needs assessment (see Figure 3.1).

If the PW/SW-PBS team's analysis indicates that the plan was implemented with integrity, the next step is to consider the impact of the intervention (see Figure 7.5 for a diagram of this decision-making process). Conversely, if the PW/SW-PBS team's analysis indicates that the plan was not implemented with integrity, then the team needs to consider why implementation with integrity did not occur. Again, the team has many options for collecting this information. The team can use a team-generated survey, hold individual or group interviews with predetermined staff and children, or observe the routines in question to determine conditions that hinder implementation. Once the reasons for lack of implementation have been determined, the team has to consider whether retooling is a viable option or whether the intervention itself needs to be shelved until more commitment is established or abandoned because it is not viable for implementation at the present time. An example of this process follows on page 105.

Figure 7.5   Data decision-making process

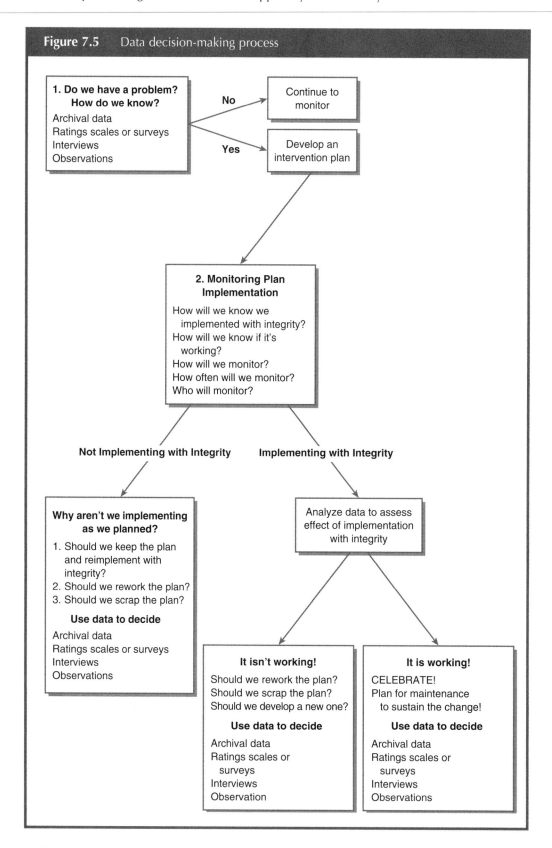

They Don't Like the Playground Rules

An SW-PBS team had questions pertaining to whether or not the routines and rules for the playground were consistently implemented as planned. ODR data indicated that referrals from the playground were consistently higher than any other location in the school, even with a new playground intervention. The team developed a survey that focused on the agreed-on rules and routines for the playground. The team asked staff to indicate whether they agreed with each rule or routine, whether they taught each of them to their students, and whether they enforced and reinforced the rules and routines while supervising on the playground. On analysis of the survey results, the team realized that there was lingering staff disagreement about some of the proposed rules and routines. For the rules and routines that proved to be more contentious, based on the survey, the PBS team decided to approach staff representing each of the grade levels for further discussion. Following these discussions, the building eventually came to consensus, on a revised playground plan. Lessons for all staff were tweaked to match the revised plan, signs leading to the playground were redone and reposted, and roles for staff who had supervisory duties were redistributed. The entire staff reimplemented the revised plan for four weeks, and the PBS team took observational data to confirm that the plan was being implemented with integrity. At this point, the team was ready to assess the impact of the newly revised plan.

Determining the Impact of Interventions. After the PW/SW-PBS team determines that an intervention has been implemented with integrity, it is ready to assess the outcomes of the intervention using multiple sources of data. The team needs to use data at every PBS meeting to guide ongoing program implementation and refinement. Data monitoring between PBS meetings is highly recommended if meetings are held fewer than two times per month. As stated earlier, in most cases, determining whether the impact of interventions is positive or meaningful is frequently dependent on programwide or schoolwide criteria. If the impact has not been as positive as anticipated (e.g., office referrals from the playground have not dropped), then the team must consider for whom and under what conditions the intervention has not yielded a positive impact and whether the plan should be reimplemented with higher integrity for certain individuals, tweaked, or reworked. If the impact has been as beneficial as anticipated (e.g., a *meaningful* decrease in office referrals from the playground), the team needs to celebrate and plan for maintenance of the intervention (see Figure 7.5).

Archival data such as ODRs or behavioral incident reports for problem behaviors are a common starting point for team data analysis of intervention impact. From ODR data teams can determine

- Times of referrals
- Locations of referrals
- Types of behaviors referred
- Possible motivations
- Individuals involved (e.g., referring staff and students)

Comparing these ODR data before and after interventions have been implemented allows teams to determine whether the changes are meaningful. In addition, team members could conduct interviews or surveys to solicit stakeholders' opinions about how the new plan is working to further assess the intervention's impact on those who are implementing the plan. The playground scenario presented earlier is now revisited with the new intervention data.

Does the New Playground Plan Work?

Once the observation data indicated that the elementary school's playground plan was implemented with integrity after it was reworked, the team had to determine whether the new plan resulted in meaningful change. An analysis of ODR data indicated that the overall level of referrals displayed a small but observable decrease. The team spread the word that the plan was working and that teachers should continue implementing the plan at the universal level. However, the data also indicated that a handful of children were still consistently displaying problem behaviors during grade-level recesses. Further data reporting for grade-level recesses indicated that a large group of first graders and two third-grade boys were the source of the majority of playground referrals. These data indicated that additional interventions were needed for all of the first-grade teachers, their first-grade students, and the two third-grade boys.

Individual Decision Making. Teams typically first focus on the impact of plan implementation from a broader perspective, at the programwide or schoolwide level, and then move toward a more narrow focus, on specific individuals. Although a thorough discussion of highly individualized data collection and decision making is beyond the scope of this text, this section provides some general information for supporting individual children but focuses more on supporting individual staff.

As with decision making for the broader context of schoolwide universals, a closer assessment at the individual level should also rely on multiple data sources. Teams can use ODRs or behavioral incident reports, observations, teacher referrals, and rating scales or surveys to identify for whom and under what conditions the universal PBS interventions are not working. The staff or students who are identified as nonresponders to the universal PBS intervention will need further support. The data should allow the team to establish whether the problem is a skill deficit or a performance deficit. As discussed in Chapter 6, a problem behavior that is a **skill deficit** means that the individual has not learned to perform the skill, and the individual will need to learn how to demonstrate the desired behavior. If the data indicate that the skill is within the individual's ability and knowledge level but he or she is not displaying the skill or does not use the skill consistently, then this is a **performance problem**. In this case, the intervention plan must include a process for prompting, providing performance feedback or incentives for compliance with expectations, and determining environmental factors that may need to be changed to support the use of the skill. Teams must plan to systematically monitor these intervention efforts with individuals and use data to determine whether improvements are made. Chapter 6 included strategies for supporting children with skill deficits by using consistent and corrective consequences. However, in many cases, staff will show deficits and need to be the target of behavior change.

Interventions based on skills or performance needs for individual staff may include peer mentoring or coaching. Peer mentoring and peer coaching are strategies that include information dissemination and training and performance support and have been proven to be effective in behavior change (Joyce & Showers, 2002). Examples of how data are used to support decision making regarding interventions and support needs for individuals follow. The first example revisits the playground scenario.

A Collaborative Effort Needed for the Playground

After an elementary PBS team identified that there were three distinct groups of individuals who needed greater support for playground problems (the first-grade teachers, their students, and two third-grade boys), the team developed intervention plans. After getting schedules of lesson plan teaching and copies of lesson plans as artifacts, it did appear that the first-grade teachers had taught the content. However, after observing the first-grade teachers' supervision on the playground, it was clear that they were not implementing key supports on the playground. The teachers were not actively moving around, prompting and acknowledging appropriate behavior, and it was not clear that they had actually taught the lessons with integrity. The team suggested a reiteration of teaching and supervision responsibilities for the first-grade teachers and identified the building principal as the team member who would be in charge of communicating this to teachers. The team also recommended a reteaching of lessons and grade level–appropriate group games for all first graders by the first-grade teachers with assistance from the gym teacher and modeling of supervision during first-grade recess by the principal. The first-grade teachers developed a feedback process for celebrating when the children demonstrated safe and responsible playground behaviors and instituted a more consistent continuum of consequences for misbehavior.

The assistant principal (AP) worked with the two third-grade boys who displayed repeated problem behaviors on the playground. The boys first practiced appropriate playground behaviors with the AP, then observed behavior during first-grade recess and gave the AP data reports, and finally role-played appropriate behaviors for the first-grade classes on the playground. The boys began to participate for limited periods of time in their grade-level recess and received daily feedback from the third-grade teachers, who served as grade-level recess playground supervisors. Both boys slowly earned third-grade recess time back and, at the end of their first full problem-free week, they received permission from the AP to retain full playground privileges as long as they remained problem free. The AP checked in weekly with the students and their teachers, who continued to give the boys ongoing performance feedback about their playground behaviors.

SUMMARY

Having a few clearly articulated questions and a specific plan for data collection and analysis enables teams to focus their efforts and be successful, data-based decision makers. The implementation of a systematic process also helps PBS teams develop and sustain effective PW/SW-PBS interventions. An efficient data collection process capitalizes on archival data readily available and also includes the identification of additional information needed to answer the questions identified. Effective data analysis follows a consistent process for comparing results of the data to goals or targets set by the team.

When teams are first implementing PW/SW-PBS, they focus their decision-making processes by assessing integrity of plan implementation and impact of interventions at the universal level. After the universal features are clearly in place, teams narrow their questions and plans toward more targeted data collection and analysis for individual planning that focuses on nonresponders to the universal interventions.

8 Building Foundations for Small-Group and Individual Supports

The primary focus of this text thus far has been on developing universal systems of positive behavior support (PBS). However, the majority of educators express concern and frustration not about the 80% of students who will respond to universal supports but about the remaining 15% to 20% of students who display chronic or intensive behavioral challenges. As outlined in Chapter 1, research suggests that approximately 10% to 15% of students within a school or program will need additional supports beyond universals to be successful. Likewise, an additional 5% to 10% will need intensive and highly individualized supports to be successful. The purpose of this chapter is to provide an overview of the necessary components to develop small-group, targeted, and individual student supports within the context of a programwide/schoolwide (PW/SW) system of supports. As with all the features discussed in this text, it is important to keep in mind that it is not simply a matter of taking examples or implementing specific behavioral interventions: **The task is to build a comprehensive system of practices guided by data decisions, with a vigilant eye toward supporting the adults in the school environment who are responsible for implementation.**

UNIVERSALS FIRMLY IN PLACE

The key to building effective behavioral supports is understanding that behavior is functionally related to the teaching environment (Lewis, Lewis-Palmer, Stichter, & Newcomer, 2004). A functional relationship simply indicates that when one event happens (e.g., the teacher prompts the class with "eyes on me" after teaching and practicing the prompt), there is a high likelihood that a predictable event will follow (e.g., the students stop what they are doing and look at the teacher). As educators we cannot *make* children behave. For that matter, we cannot *make* children learn. However, we can establish classrooms in which teachers engage in effective instruction, carefully match curriculum to students' needs and prior learning, and use effective management practices to increase the *likelihood* that students learn and increase the *likelihood* that students behave. In both cases, we have established a functional relationship between the environment (effective instruction) and student behavior (increased academic knowledge, increased use of prosocial behavior).

It is essential that everyone within the school or program understands the basic premise that behavior is functionally related to the teaching environment. Most small-group or individual strategies fail to impact problem behavior not because the intervention is faulty but rather because the teaching environment does not consistently support students' use of the targeted replacement or prosocial behavior. Stated another way, the most effective individual intervention will not change student behavior until the environment prompts, reinforces, and maintains appropriate student behavior and makes problem behavior less effective or efficient. The common misperception is that we can send students with chronic problem behaviors to specialists, and they will somehow "fix" the child and eliminate all problem behavior. Specialists can teach children alternative means to meet their needs, but until the entire school/program environment supports the alternative, students will simply fall back into prior behavior patterns. Think about instances in which you have attempted to change your own behavior, maybe a New Year's resolution to eat healthier. Most diets don't fail because the individual decides eating poorly is a better option; rather, the environment doesn't support healthy eating. Imagine how much easier it would be if vending machines sold only carrots or if that plate in the staff room were full of whole-grain granola bars instead of doughnuts.

Therefore, before schools/programs can effectively implement small-group or individual interventions, everyone in the school/program must understand that behavior is functionally related to the teaching environment. Typically, educators develop an understanding through the development and implementation of universal supports. Building effective universal systems will increase the effectiveness of small-group and individual supports. When staff observe increases in appropriate behavior and decreases in inappropriate behavior after the teaching of key skills, increased supervision, and positive feedback to children, they are developing an understanding of how behavior is functionally related to the teaching environment. It is, therefore, essential that universal supports are firmly in place before moving up the continuum of supports. At a minimum, the team should be able to answer "yes" to all of the following to increase success with small-group/individual supports:

1. The school/program has scored at least 80% on the Schoolwide Evaluation Tool (Sugai, Lewis-Palmer, Todd, & Horner, 2001; available online at www.pbis.org/tools.htm).

2. The PBS team meets on a regular basis.

3. The PBS team reviews and uses data to guide decision making on a regular basis.

4. The school/program has experienced success with universal implementation (e.g., reduction of problems on the playground after implementation of targeted playground supports).

5. The school/program supports the PBS team and understands that to support children they may have to change some of their current teaching and supervision practices.

If the team cannot answer "yes" to all of these items, our suggestion is to keep working on universal supports.

SYSTEMS TO ESTABLISH SMALL-GROUP/TARGETED SUPPORTS

Small-group/targeted supports are designed and implemented to provide a secondary level of supports. Small-group/targeted supports are matched to student need but are not highly individualized. In addition to universals, small-group strategies are implemented with a select group of children. Targeted supports are modifications made within the classroom or other environment to support select students but are likely to also benefit other students (Lewis, 2004). A range of examples of small-group/targeted strategies will be presented later in this chapter. With all facets of PW/SW-PBS, data should be used to pinpoint appropriate supports for children within your program or school. Likewise, a major focus should be on the development of systems to support small-group/ targeted strategies similar to universals. One other thought to keep in mind, as you move up the continuum of supports, is that the intensity of the practices will increase to match the intensity of student behavior. The intensity of the systems to support the practices must also increase. As teams attempt to implement small-group/targeted and individual supports, attention to detail in creating sustainable systems and connecting those systems to the larger PW/SW system is essential. The remainder of this section provides an overview of the essential features in building small-group/targeted supports.

Notify Parents. The first step in the process should be to develop a friendly and supportive notice to parents that there are concerns about their children's behavior and that a team of educators will be meeting to develop supports to allow their children to be more successful. It is also appropriate to invite the parents to the team meeting to assist in the process. This will allow additional insight into the children's behavior patterns and create the opportunity to partner with parents, increasing the likelihood of home implementation and supports.

Create a Catalog. The majority of schools/programs currently implement some level of small-group supports. For example, the school counselor might run social skills groups with a few children, or the director or assistant principal may have a few students on self-monitoring plans. However, most schools run small-group supports in isolation from a larger systemic behavior support system. Therefore, when initiating more intense levels of support, one of the first steps for the team is to catalog the practices currently in place in the school/program and the resources that are allocated to support them. Once practices are identified, the team should make an informal assessment of the effectiveness of each of the practices. A review of behavioral infractions and teacher perceptions can provide an overall view of current effectiveness. At this point, the team should also identify critical features that allow some practices to be effective and others ineffective. It is also important to understand that simply because the school/program is currently implementing a practice does not mean it will continue. The final decision to select a small-group practice will rely on student need.

Establish the "Ticket In." The next step in establishing a system at the small-group/targeted level is the development of data decision rules. The team should look to current data collected as part of their universal supports and create minimums whereby students are referred for secondary supports (i.e., the "ticket in"). For example, the team may decide, after reviewing the whole-school behavioral infraction data, that students who receive five behavioral infractions should be referred for small-group supports. Several factors should be kept in mind as the team develops its set of decision rules. First, existing data should be used when possible to build on the practice of ongoing data review established at the universal level. Second, a simple teacher referral form should also be developed as an alternative method for identifying students. Third, keep in mind that children with externalizing behaviors (e.g., acting out, noncompliant, physically aggressive) will come to the team's attention quickly through behavioral infraction data and teacher referral process. The team should also establish data reviews to identify students with internalizing behavior problems (e.g., depressed, withdrawn, socially isolated). Reviews of attendance, grades or academic/preacademic performance, and teacher referral can serve to identify students at risk because of internalizing behavior.

The PBS team should also look for data patterns that suggest the need for other types of targeted supports. If one particular classroom or setting within the program/school has a higher than average rate of behavioral infractions, targeted interventions may be appropriate. Targeted interventions are characterized as changes in classroom or setting procedures, routines, and instruction to impact at-risk student behavior. The focus within targeted interventions is typically more on the adult behavior. Targeted interventions provide strategies and supports to the adults within settings in which higher than average rates of problem behavior are occurring. Targeted supports are just that: "supports." The use of data to identify problem areas and provide assistance to teachers should be done in a caring, supportive manner, not the traditional evaluative manner in which judgments are made about good or bad teaching.

Match Student Need to Support. Following the creation of decision rules to identify students, the next step is to match student need to intervention. It is recommended that teams consider three broad areas of need: **social behavior needs**, **academic/preacademic skill deficits**, and **social-emotional needs**. For social behavior needs, the data indicate a pattern of disruptive, noncompliant, or problematic peer interaction behavior patterns. Regarding academic/preacademic skill deficits, although students may be identified based on behavioral patterns, when evaluated, a pattern of association between problem behavior and academic/preacademic skills is apparent. In the final broad category of need, social-emotional, students may not be displaying high rates of problem behavior, but concerns are expressed through teacher referral or other data sources (e.g., increased absences, withdrawal from peers).

Table 8.1   Examples of Interventions Matched to Student Needs

Need area based on examination of data	Small-group/Targeted intervention
Social-behavioral	• Social skills club
	• Self-management
Academic/preacademic	• Homework club
	• Tutoring
	• Peer tutoring
	• Check in/check out
	• Instructional modifications
Social-emotional	• Mentors
	• Service club

Complex assessments or evaluations are not necessary at this level of behavioral support. Teams are encouraged to review existing data, teacher input, and archival information (e.g., past successful supports) to determine need areas. The second step at this level is to match the intervention to the need. Table 8.1 provides an overview of common interventions matched to need areas. More detailed information about these practices is presented later in this chapter.

Regardless of the intervention selected, all activities should be directly linked back to the school/program expectations. For example, in a social skills club, the focus might be on anger management, but the language within the lessons should connect back to the program/school expectation of "Respecting others." Alternatively, within the peer-tutoring sessions, the emphasis is on achieving academic outcomes, and this is tied to the school expectation "Being a learner."

Provide Training and Support to Implementers. Central to the establishment of universal supports is to assume students do not know what to do and teach them. The same holds true for staff who will take a lead role in implementing small-group/targeted supports: Do not assume they will know what to do. Tap expertise both within and outside the school/program to assist in the design, implementation, and evaluation features of all small-group strategies. In addition, ensure that those who are directly responsible for the implementation of the strategy have been trained to do so and can access ongoing technical assistance to guarantee a high-quality intervention. It is also critical to success that everyone on staff receive training on the strategy to the point of achieving a basic understanding of the strategy and the intended outcomes. The PBS team's task is to build a connected continuum, not to replicate a piecemeal approach to service delivery.

Provide Follow-Along Activities. Once implementation of the small-group strategy has begun, follow-along activities should be shared with classroom teachers and other staff who interact with the students on a daily basis. The key to promoting successful maintenance and generalization of outcomes is to provide the adults in the teaching environment with clear directions regarding their roles. For example, if eight students meet once a week to receive social skills instruction targeting anger management and conflict resolution, after each session, classroom teachers and others should receive a quick overview of what was covered in the lesson and two to three ways they can prompt, practice, and acknowledge the skills in their classroom and other school/program settings.

Monitor and Evaluate. Before starting any small-group support, a plan to monitor and evaluate outcomes should be established. Within the plan, three targets should be established: (a) student outcomes, (b) teacher/staff perceptions of improvement, and (c) cost–benefit evaluation. Outcomes such as reductions in behavioral infractions, increased time spent in the classroom as a result of fewer removals caused by problem behavior, attendance, and achievement are all simple measures that should be collected as part of the larger PW/SW system and can be used to monitor individual student progress. Simple surveys or interviews of staff directly responsible for implementation and those who work with the students throughout the day can also provide valuable input. Finally, a comparison of student outcomes to staff time should be undertaken to assess cost–benefit with an eye toward maximizing efficiencies. Are there simpler, less intensive practices and supports that could have been put in place to reach the same or similar outcomes?

Provide Long-Term Supports. A common mistake educators often make is withdrawing supports too soon after behavioral improvement. Student data will indicate when supports are withdrawn too early through increases in rates of problem behavior displayed by the targeted students. To increase the likelihood of maintaining behavioral improvements, teams should incorporate three strategies within all small-group/targeted interventions. First, as mentioned previously, all small-group supports should be tied directly to the larger PW/SW expectations, routines, teaching practices, and feedback practices. By linking to the larger PW/SW system, students will continue to receive ongoing support. Second, a self-management strategy should be built into all supports to give students strategies to monitor and maintain their own behavior change. Finally, consider involving "graduates" of small-group supports in future interventions. For example, students who have received small-group social skills instruction over the course of a school year can be enlisted to serve as teaching assistants the following year. By keeping students connected in the new role, they (a) continue to receive practice opportunities, (b) continue to receive feedback on skill use, and (c) can serve as models for younger students, especially within settings with minimal adult supervision (e.g., playgrounds).

Write It All Down. It is strongly recommended that teams codify small-group practices in two ways. First, general procedures for identifying students and the process to place and support students in small groups, plus the staff's role across all small-group supports, should be included in the PW/SW-PBS plan. Implementation checks should also be included in the general plan to ensure high integrity of implementation. Implementation checks are simple tools that allow the team to monitor the delivery of the small-group supports to ensure that the intervention is being implemented as planned. These tools can be as simple as a self-checklist completed by the implementer or a brief observation during the small-group activity.

Second, for each child receiving small-group supports, brief overviews noting plan components should be written and shared with all staff who directly work with the child as well as with the parents. A master copy should be kept with the team. The following list provides the minimum amount of information that should be included in each plan:

1. Desired outcome of small-group/targeted support.

2. Brief summary of the intervention.

3. How often small group will meet and with whom.

4. Measurement and monitoring plan with schedule.

5. Strategies to support student across all school environments.

SMALL-GROUP/TARGETED STRATEGIES

Throughout this text, we have emphasized that schools/programs must develop their own universal supports to match their presenting challenges and current resources. We have also emphasized the importance of both local development and close adherence to lessons learned through research-validated practices. The same holds true at the small-group/targeted level of support. The following are offered as examples of secondary supports along with key features. Readers are encouraged to consult other resources providing more comprehensive descriptions of small-group strategies to assist in development (Figure 8.1).

Social Skills. Small-group social skills instruction follows the same general format reviewed in this text for the universal level. Additional considerations for small-group instruction include the following (Sugai & Lewis, 1996):

1. Groups should be kept to a maximum of six to eight students.

2. It is critical to establish an attention signal and other group rules before starting social skills instruction to allow the instructors to focus on the skills versus managing behavior.

3. Social skills lessons can be taken from published curricula but must be adapted to reflect program/school rules and expectations.

4. Each lesson should follow the "tell-show-practice" format. First, the instructor states the rule for the skill (e.g., "When you get angry, the first thing you do is stop"). Second, the instructor demonstrates a range of appropriate skills, along with a couple of inappropriate skills, to show students what the skill looks like. Finally, the instructor should have the students practice using the skill through role-playing.

5. Students should be prompted for taught skills before problem times or settings and reinforced when they display the learned social skills across time and settings.

Self-Management. Ideally, self-management strategies are embedded in all small-group and individual supports. Self-management practices have two essential features: (a) self-monitoring and (b) self-reinforcement. Self-monitoring is the process of tuning into one's own behavior and recording outcomes. Self-monitoring can range from simple evaluations at the end of a period (e.g., circle smiling or frowning faces related to staying on task) to timed intervals in which a tone signals the students to mark how well they are meeting behavioral targets (e.g., tone every five minutes, students mark a plus sign or minus sign on a chart attached to their desk). Self-reinforcement is the process of accessing desired outcomes if minimum behavioral criteria (via self-monitoring) are met. Self-management must be actively taught and monitored until students develop fluency. Self-management is typically taught through the following steps.

Figure 8.1   Additional resources for small-group/targeted and individual systems

Targeted Group/Small Group

Crone, D. A., Horner, R. H., & Hawken, L. S. (2004). *Responding to problem behavior in schools: The Behavior Education Program.* New York: Guilford Press.

Hawken, L. S., Horner, R. H. (2003). Evaluation of a targeted intervention within a schoolwide system of behavior support. *Journal of Behavioral Education, 12*(3), 225–240.

Lewis, T. J., & Newcomer, L. L. (2002). Examining the efficacy of school-based consultation: Recommendations for improving outcomes. In J. K. Luiselli & C. Diament (Eds.), *Behavior psychology in the schools* (pp. 165–181). New York: Hawthorne Press.

Todd, A., Horner, R., & Sugai, G. (1999). Self-monitoring and self-recruited praise: Effects on problem behavior, academic engagement, and work completion in a typical classroom. *Journal of Positive Behavior Interventions, 1*(2), 66–76.

Todd, A., Horner, R., Sugai, G., & Colvin, G. (1999). Individualizing school-wide discipline for students with chronic problem behaviors: A team approach. *Effective School Practices, 17*(4), 72–82.

Individual Systems

Bambara, L.M., & Kern, L., Eds. (2005). *Individualized supports for students with problem behaviors: Designing positive behavior plans.* New York: Guilford Press.

Crone, D., & Horner, R. H. (2003). *Building positive behavior support systems in schools: Functional behavioral assessment.* New York: Guilford Press.

Freeman, R., Baker, D., Horner, R., Smith, C., Britten, J., & McCart, A. (2002). Using functional assessment and systems-level assessment to build effective behavioral support plans. In R. H. Hanson, N. A. Wieseler, & K. C. Lakin (Eds.), *Crisis: Prevention and response in the community* (pp. 199–224). Washington, DC: American Association on Mental Retardation.

Horner, R. H., Sugai, G., Todd, A. W., & Lewis-Palmer, T. (1999–2000). Elements of behavior support plans: A technical brief. *Exceptionality, 8*(3), 205–215.

Lewis, T. J., Newcomer, L., Kelk, M., & Powers, L. (2000). One youth at a time: Addressing aggression and violence through individual systems of positive behavioral support. *Reaching Today's Youth, 5*(1), 37–41.

March, R., Horner, R. H., Lewis-Palmer, T., Brown, D., Crone, D. A., Todd, A., & Carr, E. (2000). *Functional Assessment Checklist for Teachers and Staff* (FACTS). Retrieved June 1, 2006, from http://www.pbis.org/tools.htm

Newcomer, L. L., & Lewis, T. J. (2002, December 15). Building connections between individual behavior support plans and schoolwide systems of positive behavior support. *Positive Behavioral Supports & Interventions Newsletter, 1*(4). Retrieved from http://www.pbis.org/news

Snell, M. E., Voorhees, M. D., & Chen, L.Y. (2005). Team involvement in assessment-based interventions with problem behavior: 1997–2002. *Journal of Positive Behavior Interventions, 7*(3), 140–152.

Sugai, G., Horner, R. H., Dunlap, G., Hieneman, M., Lewis, T. J., Nelson, C. M., et al. (2000). Applying positive behavior support and functional behavioral assessment in schools. *Journal of Positive Behavior Interventions, 2*(3), 131–143.

1. The student is taught the target or desired behavior using social skills instruction.

2. The student is taught how to use the self-monitoring tool.

3. The teacher and student practice completing the self-monitoring tool during brief trials, discussing outcomes and addressing why and how criteria were or were not met.

4. The student practices using self-monitoring while the teacher simultaneously monitors. Training continues until a student accuracy of 80% or better is achieved compared with the teacher's rating.

5. The student is reinforced for (a) accurate self-monitoring and (b) demonstrating the appropriate targeted behavior. It is important to highlight successful displays of appropriate behavior and not simply correct monitoring because this is the ultimate outcome of the strategy.

6. The student uses self-monitoring tools during targeted times with periodic teacher checks for accuracy. The student can access outcomes for meeting predetermined criteria (self-reinforcement).

Academic/Preacademic Supports. Problem behavior is often displayed during academic/preacademic periods. Academic supports can take several forms, ranging from specialist support (e.g., literacy specialist) to an increase in tutoring to peer tutoring. Across each of these supports, the focus should be on providing students with the needed academic assistance and teaching them how to access assistance appropriately.

Mentoring/Connecting to At-Risk Students. Many students may be displaying inappropriate behavior as a result of daily inconsistencies in their personal lives or major events such as a divorce in the family. In addition, research has demonstrated the clear link between consistent, caring adults in children's lives and later life outcomes. Therefore, many schools have established mentoring programs as a means to connect with at-risk children and provide some stability in their otherwise often chaotic lives. Mentors are not established to serve as counselors or as friends but rather as adults who are available to the children on a consistent basis and demonstrate caring through interest in the children's lives. It is recommended that mentors be matched to students through mutual selection, and mentors be selected from within program/school staff to ensure consistency and availability. Other recommendations include the following:

1. Administrators are not eligible to mentor given their role as an authority figure.

2. Students and teachers within the same classroom should not be matched.

3. Staff agree to meet at least once a week for a minimum of ten minutes.

4. Staff are not to nag children about schoolwork; they should simply get to know the children and talk with them about their lives.

5. Staff are not required to take students to outings outside the school day.

These guidelines are offered as minimums to ensure a clear focus and to make mentoring manageable.

Targeted Supports. Targeted supports are defined as changes in the environment in response to student need that are designed to increase appropriate behavior. For example, a child with attention problems may be creating several disruptions in class. Through an environmental assessment, recommendations related to classroom routines or consistent use of attention procedures are given to the teacher along with information, training, and ongoing support and feedback as a means to reduce problem behavior displayed by the child. The following are general steps used in implementing targeted supports (Stichter, Lewis, Richter, Johnson, & Bradley, 2006):

1. Conduct an environmental assessment and match to research recommendations related to effective instruction (see Cotton, 1999).

2. Provide information and support to the classroom teacher and other staff through brief training, tip sheets with key skills, and ongoing assistance through consultation or peer coaching.

3. Monitor both student and staff behavior. If student behavior is not improving, first check to ensure that staff are implementing recommended changes consistently.

INTENSIVE/INDIVIDUAL STUDENT SUPPORTS

The final level of the continuum of supports focuses on those students who display significant patterns of problem behavior or who have not responded to universal and small-group supports. In addition to school-based supports, related supports such as mental health or family services are often coordinated at this level. As with the small groups, the key is linking supports at this level back to the PW/SW rules, expectations, and routines. A thorough review of the necessary features at the individual level is beyond the scope of this text, and readers are encouraged to seek more detailed and focused information related to the essential features of individual supports.

As the name implies, supports at this level should be highly individualized based on student need. However, all school/program teams should develop a system for identifying and supporting individual students along with a clear process that delineates roles and responsibilities and follows current recommended best practices. For purposes of discussion within this section, the primary focus is on social behavior issues. Teams are also encouraged to develop clear support processes for academic concerns that are also linked to PW/SW behavior supports.

The cornerstone of developing school-based individual behavior supports is applying the "key" premise (i.e., behavior is functionally related to the teaching environment) in an organized and systemic manner through the process of functional behavior assessment (FBA). To ensure success, school/program teams must have

1. Someone with expertise and fluency in conducting FBAs,

2. A clear process in which all staff understand their role and outcomes, and

3. A basic understanding among all staff that the environment must support individual student prosocial behavior (Lewis & Lewis, 2006).

The basic logic of conducting an FBA is built on the principles that (a) problem behavior allows students to get their needs met and (b) behavior communicates those needs. In other words, FBAs are conducted to figure out why children engage in problem behavior. FBAs provide an opportunity to examine events that precede and follow sequences of problem behavior. Based on FBA data, hypotheses are developed about what needs are being met through the problem behavior. At present, research confirms two primary purposes of problem behavior: to obtain what the child finds reinforcing and to avoid what the child finds aversive. For example, children may disrupt class to get teacher and peer attention. They may also disrupt class to be removed from the setting in which they are presented with a task they find aversive (e.g., writing).

Once a hypothesis about the purpose of the behavior is developed and confirmed through the FBA, an individual PBS plan is developed and includes three critical features:

- First, the child is taught a prosocial or appropriate way to get their needs met (e.g., raise hand for teacher attention or ask for help with a difficult task).
- Second, the targeted skill must be as or more efficient than the problem behavior in meeting the child's needs.
- Finally, the environment must not allow the problem behavior to meet the child's needs while ensuring that the newly learned skill does efficiently meet the need.

The first and second features are relatively straightforward and easy to accomplish. However, without the final step in place, it can be safely assumed that the behavior will not change. Consider this: If a child has a learning history with getting needs met with the problem behavior, why use the replacement? The child will use the replacement, or appropriate, behavior if the environment allows his or her needs to be met (e.g., teacher attends as soon as the child raises hand) and does not allow the old behavior "to work anymore." As stated at the outset of this chapter, educators cannot make a child behave; they can, however, create environments to increase the likelihood that the child will behave. By focusing on the function of the problem behavior and teaching functional-equivalent appropriate behavior, the likelihood is increased. Further, by nesting the targeted appropriate behavior within the universal system of support, the likelihood that the environment will respond to the child in a consistent and efficient manner is increased.

For those schools/programs beginning PBS, time is best spent on developing and implementing universal supports to lay the foundation to maximize outcomes of small-group and individual interventions by establishing a responsive, flexible, and supportive learning environment. The following list presents minimal features of an FBA-PBS process (Lewis & Lewis, 2006).

1. Teacher makes a request for assistance (standard form and submission process).

2. At the team/process meeting, (a) problem behavior and the replacement behavior are operationally defined; (b) background, archival, and environmental assessment data are reviewed to discern patterns; (c) FBA data are reviewed and include both indirect measures (e.g., rating scales, interviews) and direct observation; (d) a hypothesis is developed regarding function of problem behavior; (e) a PBS plan is developed based on function and includes social skills instruction to teach replacement behavior, environmental modifications, and scripts for adults.

3. The team implements, monitors, and evaluates the progress of the plan.

CONCLUSION

This chapter provided basic and essential steps in the development of secondary and tertiary (individual) levels of supports. Important ideas to keep in mind as teams establish a complete continuum include the following: (a) All levels of support are directly related to universal expectations, (b) an instructional approach is emphasized at every level, and (c) small-group and individual supports generally fail not because of ineffective practices but because of a breakdown in consistent systems of implementation.

References

Alberto, P., & Troutman, A. C. (2003). *Applied behavior analysis for teachers* (6th ed.). Upper Saddle River, NJ: Merrill/Prentice Hall.

Bambara, L. M., & Kern, L. (2005). *Individualized supports for students with problem behaviors: Designing positive behavior plans.* New York: Guilford.

Boudah, D. J., Logan, K. R., & Greenwood, C. R. (2001). The research to practice projects: Lessons learned about changing teacher practice. *Teacher Education and Special Education, 24*(4), 290–303.

Colvin, G., Sugai, G., Good, R. H. I., & Lee, Y. (1997). Using active supervision and precorrection to improve transition behavior in elementary school. *School Psychology Quarterly, 12*(4), 344–363.

Conduct Problems Prevention Research Group. (1992). A developmental and clinical model for the prevention of conduct disorders: The FAST Track Program. *Development and Psychopathology, 4,* 509–527.

Cotton, K. (1999). *Research you can use to improve results.* Alexandria, VA: Association for Supervision and Curriculum Development.

Covington-Smith, S. (2004). *The effects of targeted positive behavior support strategies on preschoolers' externalizing behavior.* Unpublished doctoral dissertation, University of Missouri–Columbia.

Elliot, D. S. (1994a). Serious violent offenders: Onset, developmental course, and termination—The American Society of Criminology 1993 Presidential Address. *Criminology, 32,* 1–21.

Elliot, D. S. (1994b). *Youth violence: An overview.* Boulder, CO: Center for the Study and Prevention of Violence.

Greenwood, C. R., & Abbott, M. (2001). The research to practice gap in special education. *Teacher Education and Special Education, 24*(4), 276–289.

Gresham, F. M., Sugai, G., & Horner, R. H. (2001). Interpreting outcomes of social skill training for students with high incidence disabilities. *Exceptional Children, 67,* 331–344.

Guskey, T. R. (2000). *Evaluating professional development.* Thousand Oaks, CA: Corwin Press.

Hawken, L. S., & Horner, R. H. (2003). Evaluation of a targeted intervention within a schoolwide system of behavior support. *Journal of Behavioral Education, 12*(3), 225–240.

Hawley, W. D., & Valli, L. (1999). The essentials of effective professional development: A new consensus. In L. Darling-Hammond & G. Sykes (Eds.), *Teaching as a learning profession* (pp. 127–150). San Francisco: Jossey-Bass.

Heaviside, S., Rowand, C., Williams, C., & Farris, E. (1998). *Violence and discipline problems in U.S. public schools: 1996–97* (NCES Publication No. 98–030). Washington, DC: U.S. Department of Education, National Center for Education Statistics.

Horner, R. H., & Sugai, G. (2005). School-wide positive behavior support: An alternative approach to discipline in schools. In L. Bambara & L. Kern (Eds.), *Positive behavior support* (pp. 359–390). New York: Guilford.

Ingram, K. (2002). *Comparing effectiveness of intervention strategies that are based on functional behavioral assessment information and those that are contra-indicated by the assessment.* Unpublished doctoral dissertation, University of Oregon (Eugene).

Joyce, B. R., & Showers, B. (2002). *Student achievement through staff development* (3rd ed.). Alexandria, VA: Association for Supervision and Curriculum Development.

Kamps, D., Kravits, T., Rauch, J., Kamps, J. L., & Chung, N. (2000). A prevention program for students with or at risk of ED: Moderating effects of variation in treatment and classroom structure. *Journal of Emotional and Behavioral Disorders, 8*(3), 141–154.

Kamps, D., Kravits, T., Stolze, J., & Swaggart, B. (1999). Prevention strategies for at-risk students and students with EBD in urban elementary schools. *Journal of Emotional and Behavioral Disorders, 7*(3), 178–189.

Kartub, D. T., Taylor-Greene, S., March, R. E., & Horner, R. H. (2000). Reducing hallway noise: A systems approach. *Journal of Positive Behavior Interventions, 2,* 179–182.

Kauffman, J. M. (1993). How we might achieve the radical reform of special education. *Exceptional Children, 60,* 6–16.

Kauffman, J. M. (2005). *Characteristics of emotional and behavioral disorders of children and youth* (8th ed.). Upper Saddle River, NJ: Prentice Hall.

Klinger, J. K., Ahwee, S., Piloneta, P., & Menendez, R. (2003). Barriers and facilitators in scaling up research-based practices. *Exceptional Children, 69*(4), 411–429.

Klinger, J. K., Arguelles, M. E., Hughes, M. T., & Vaughn, S. (2001). Examining the schoolwide "spread" of research-based practices. *Learning Disability Quarterly, 24,* 221–234.

Koop, C. E., & Lundberg, G. (1992). Violence in America: A public health emergency: Time to bite the bullet back. *Journal of the American Medical Association, 267,* 3075–3076.

Kupersmidt, J. B., Bryant, D., & Willoughby, M. T. (2000). Prevalence of aggressive behaviors among preschoolers in Head Start and community child care programs. *Behavioral Disorders, 26,* 42–52.

Lampi, A. R., Fenty, N. S., & Beaunae, C. (2005). Making the three Ps easier: Praise, proximity, and precorrection. *Beyond Behavior, 15,* 8–12.

Langland, S., Lewis-Palmer, T., & Sugai, G. (1998). Teaching respect in the classroom: An instructional approach. *Journal of Behavioral Education, 8,* 245–262.

Lewis, T. J. (2004, October). *Developing small group supports within a continuum of school-wide positive behavior supports.* Paper presented at the Annual School-wide PBS Implementation Forum, Chicago.

Lewis, T. J., Colvin, G., & Sugai, G. (2000). The effects of precorrection and active supervision on the recess behavior of elementary school students. *Education and Treatment of Children, 23,* 109–121.

Lewis, T. J., & Lewis, L. (2006, October). *Essential features of individual systems of support: Data, practices, and systems.* Paper presented at the 3rd Annual School-wide PBS Implementation Forum, Chicago.

Lewis, T. J., Lewis-Palmer, T., Stichter, J., & Newcomer, L. L. (2004). Applied behavior analysis and the education and treatment of students with emotional and behavioral disorders. In R. Rutherford, M. M. Quinn, & S. Mathur (Eds.), *Handbook of research in behavioral disorders* (pp. 523–545). New York: Guilford.

Lewis, T. J., & Newcomer, L. L. (2002). Examining the efficacy of school-based consultation: Recommendations for improving outcomes. *Child and Family Behavior Therapy, 24,* 165–181.

Lewis, T. J., Newcomer, L., Trussell, R., & Richter, M. (2006). School-wide positive behavior support: Building systems to develop and maintain appropriate social behavior. In C. S. Everston & C. M. Weinstein (Eds.), *Handbook of classroom management: Research, practice and contemporary issues* (pp. 833–854). New York: Lawrence Erlbaum.

Lewis, T. J., Powers, L. J., Kelk, M. J., & Newcomer, L. (2002). Reducing problem behaviors on the playground: An investigation of the application of school-wide positive behavior supports. *Psychology in the Schools, 39,* 181–190.

Lewis, T. J., & Sugai, G. (1999). Effective behavior support: A systems approach to proactive school-wide management. *Focus on Exceptional Children, 31*(6), 1–24.

Lewis, T. J, Sugai, G., & Colvin, G. (1998). Reducing problem behavior through a school-wide system of effective behavioral support: Investigation of a school-wide social skills training program and contextual interventions. *School Psychology Review, 27,* 446–459.

Lewis-Palmer, T., Sugai, G., & Larson, S. (1999). Using data to guide decisions about program implementation and effectiveness: An overview and applied example. *Effective School Practices, 17*(4), 1–7.

Mayer, G. R. (1995). Preventing antisocial behavior in the schools. *Journal of Applied Behavior Analysis, 28,* 467–478.

Mayer, G. R. (2001). Antisocial behavior: Its causes and prevention within our schools. *Education & Treatment of Children, 24,* 414–429.

Meese, R. (2001). *Teaching learners with mild disabilities* (2nd ed.). Belmont, CA: Wadsworth.

Mercer, C. D., & Mercer, A. R. (2005). *Teaching students with learning problems* (7th ed.). Upper Saddle River, NJ: Pearson/Merrill/Prentice Hall.

Missouri Positive Behavior Support Initiative. (2002). *Training manual for introduction and overview of PBS.* Columbia: University of Missouri Center for Positive Behavior Supports.

Myers, C. L., & Holland, K. L. (2000). Classroom behavioral interventions: Do teachers consider the function of the behavior? *Psychology in the Schools, 37*(3), 271–280.

Nakasato, J. (2000). Data-based decision making in Hawaii's behavior support effort. *Journal of Positive Behavior Interventions, 2*(4), 247–251.

Newcomer, L., & Lewis, T. (2004). Functional behavioral assessment: An investigation of assessment reliability and effectiveness of function-based interventions. *Journal of Emotional and Behavioral Disorders, 12*(3), 168–181.

Newcomer, L., & Powers, L. (2002, February). *A team approach to functional behavioral assessment-based positive behavioral support plans.* Paper presented at the Midwest Symposium for Leadership in Behavior Disorders, Kansas City, MO.

Odom, S. L., McConnell, S. R., & McEvoy, M. A. (1992). Peer-related social competence and its significance for young children. In S. L. Odom, S. R. McConnell, & M. A. McEvoy (Eds.), *Social competence of young children with disabilities: Issues and strategies for intervention* (pp. 3–36). Baltimore, MD: Paul H. Brookes.

OSEP Center on Positive Behavioral Interventions and Supports. (2004). *Schoolwide positive behavior support: Implementers' blueprint and self-assessment.* Eugene, OR: Author.

Patterson, G. R. (1982). *A social learning approach: Coercive family process.* Eugene, OR: Castalia Press.

Peacock Hill Working Group. (1991). Problems and promises in special education and related services for children and youth with emotional and behavioral disorders. *Behavioral Disorders, 16,* 299–313.

Platt, A. D., Tripp, C. E., Ogden, W. R., & Fraser, R. G. (2000). *The skillful leader: Confronting mediocre teaching.* Acton, MA: Ready About Press.

Powers, L. J. (2003). *Examining effects of targeted group social skills intervention in schools with and without school-wide systems of positive behavior support.* Unpublished doctoral dissertation, University of Missouri–Columbia.

Putnam, R. F., Handler, M. W., Ramirez-Platt, C., & Luiselli, J. K. (2003). Improving student bus-riding behavior through a whole-school intervention. *Journal of Applied Behavior Analysis, 36,* 583–590.

Rosenshine, B., & Stevens, R. (1986). Teaching functions. In M. C. Wittrock (Ed.), *Handbook of research in teaching* (3rd ed., pp. 376–391). New York: Macmillan.

Safran, S. P., & Oswald, K. (2003). Positive behavior supports: Can schools reshape disciplinary practices? *Exceptional Children, 69,* 361–373.

Scott, T. M. (2001). A school-wide example of positive behavioral support. *Journal of Positive Behavioral Interventions, 3,* 88–94.

Scott, T. M., & Martinek, G. (2006). Coaching positive behavior support in school settings: Tactics and data-based decision making. *Journal of Positive Behavior Interventions, 8*(3), 165–173.

Serna, L., Nielsen, E., Lambros, K., & Forness, S. (2000). Primary prevention with children at risk for emotional or behavioral disorders: Data on a universal intervention for Head Start classrooms. *Behavioral Disorders, 26*(1), 70–84.

Skinner, C. H., Neddenriep, C. E., Robinson, S. L., Ervin, R., & Jones, K. (2002). Altering educational environments through positive peer reporting: Prevention and remediation of social problems associated with behavior disorders. *Psychology in the Schools, 39*(2), 191–202.

Stichter, J. P., & Lewis, T. J. (2005, March). *Classroom variables related to effective literacy instruction: Implications for targeted interventions within school-wide PBS systems.* Paper presented at the International Conference on Positive Behavior Support, Tampa, FL.

Stichter, J. P., Lewis, T. J., Johnson, N., & Trussell, R. (2004). Toward a structural assessment: Analyzing the merits of an assessment tool for a student with E/BD. *Assessment for Effective Intervention, 30,* 25–40.

Stichter, J. P., Lewis, T. J., Richter, M., Johnson, N. W., & Bradley, L. (2006). Assessing antecedent variables: The effects of instructional variables on student outcomes through in-service and peer coaching professional development models. *Education & Treatment of Children, 29*(4), 665–692.

Stormont, M. (2007). *Fostering resilience in young children vulnerable for failure: Strategies for K–3.* Columbus, OH: Pearson/Merrill/Prentice Hall.

Stormont, M., Beckner, R., Mitchell, B., & Richter, M. (2005). Supporting successful transition to kindergarten: General challenges and specific implications for students with problem behavior. *Psychology in the Schools, 42,* 765–778.

Stormont, M., Covington, S., & Lewis, T. J. (2006). Using data to inform systems: Assessing teacher implementation of key features of positive behavior support. *Beyond Behavior, 15*(3), 10–14.

Stormont, M., Lewis, T. J., & Beckner, B. (2005). Developmentally continuous positive behavior support systems: Applying key features in preschool settings. *Teaching Exceptional Children, 37,* 42–48.

Stormont, M., Lewis, T. J., & Covington, S. (2005). Behavior support strategies in early childhood settings: Teachers' importance and feasibility ratings. *Journal of Positive Behavior Interventions, 7,* 131–139.

Stormont, M., Smith, S. C., & Lewis, T. J. (in press). Teacher implementation of precorrection and praise statements in Head Start classrooms as a component of a program-wide system of positive behavior support. *Journal of Behavioral Education.*

Sugai, G., & Horner, R. (1996). *Antisocial behavior, discipline and behavioral support: A look from the schoolhouse door.* Unpublished manuscript, University of Oregon.

Sugai, G., Horner, R. H., Dunlap, G., Hieneman, M., Lewis, T. J., Nelson, C. M., et al. (2000). *Applying positive behavioral support and functional behavioral assessment in schools.* Washington, DC: OSEP Center on Positive Behavioral Interventions and Supports.

Sugai, G., Horner, R., Lewis, T. J., & Cheney, D. (2002, July). *Positive behavioral supports.* Paper presented at the OSEP Research Project Directors' Conference, Washington, D.C.

Sugai, G., & Lewis, T. (1996). Preferred and promising practices for social skill instruction. *Focus on Exceptional Children, 29*(4), 1–16.

Sugai, G., Lewis-Palmer, T., Todd, A., & Horner, R. H. (2001). *School-wide evaluation tool version 2.0.* Retrieved June 1, 2006, from http://www.pbis.org/tools.htm

Sugai, G. M., & Tindal, G. (1993). *Effective school consultation: An interactive approach.* Pacific Grove, CA: Brooks/Cole.

Tankersley, M., Kamps, D., Mancina, C., & Weidinger, D. (1996). Social interventions for Head Start children with behavioral risks: Implementation and outcomes. *Journal of Emotional and Behavioral Disorders, 4,* 171–181.

Taylor-Greene, S., Brown, D. K., Nelson, L., Longton, J., Gassman, T., Cohen, J., et al. (1997). School-wide behavioral support: Starting the year off right. *Journal of Behavioral Education, 7,* 99–112.

Taylor-Greene, S. J., & Kartub, D. T. (2000). Durable implementation of school-wide positive behavior support: The High Five Program. *Journal of Positive Behavior Interventions, 2,* 233–235.

Tobin, T. J., & Sugai, G. M. (1999). Discipline problems, placements, and outcomes for students with serious emotional disturbance. *Behavioral Disorders, 24*(2), 109–121.

Tobin, T., Sugai, G., & Colvin, G. (1996). Patterns in middle school discipline referrals. *Journal of Emotional and Behavioral Disorders, 4*(2), 82–94.

Todd, A. W., Haugen, L., Anderson, K., & Spriggs, M. (2002). Teaching recess: Low-cost efforts producing effective results. *Journal of Positive Behavior Interventions, 4*(1), 46–52.

Tolan, P., & Guerra, N. (1994). *What works in reducing adolescent violence: An empirical review of the field.* Boulder, CO: Center for the Study and Prevention of Violence.

Turnbull, A., Turnbull, R., Erwin, E., & Soodak, L. (2006). *Families, professionals, and exceptionality: Positive outcome through partnerships and trust* (5th ed.). Upper Saddle River, NJ: Pearson/Merrill/Prentice Hall.

Walker, H. M., Colvin, G., & Ramsey, E. (1995). *Antisocial behavior in school: Strategies and best practices.* Pacific Grove, CA: Brooks/Cole.

Walker, H. M., Horner, R., Sugai, G., Bullis, M., Sprague, J., Bricker, D., & Kaufman, J. (1996). Integrated approaches to preventing antisocial behavior patterns among school-age children and youth. *Journal of Emotional and Behavioral Disorders, 4,* 193–256.

Walker, H. M., Ramsey, E., & Gresham, F. M. (2004). *Antisocial behavior in school: Evidence-based practices* (2nd ed.). Belmont, CA: Thomson-Wadsworth.

Webster-Stratton, C. (1997). Treating children with early-onset conduct problems: A comparison of child and parent training interventions. *Journal of Consulting Clinical Psychology, 65,* 93–109.

Willoughby, M., Kupersmidt, J., & Bryant, D. (2001). Overt and covert dimensions of antisocial behavior in early childhood. *Journal of Abnormal Child Psychology, 29*(3), 177–187.

Zentall, S. S. (2006). *ADHD and education: Foundations, characteristics, methods, and collaboration.* Upper Saddle River, NJ: Pearson/Merrill/Prentice Hall.

Index

**CORWIN
PRESS**

The Corwin Press logo—a raven striding across an open book—represents the union of courage and learning. Corwin Press is committed to improving education for all learners by publishing books and other professional development resources for those serving the field of PreK–12 education. By providing practical, hands-on materials, Corwin Press continues to carry out the promise of its motto: **"Helping Educators Do Their Work Better."**